PRAISE FOR *DECENT PEOPLE, DECENT COMPANY*

"Insightful and practical, *Decent People, Decent Company* focuses on the critical importance of character as well as competence, and it offers a richly rewarding reading experience no matter where you are on the learning curve of leadership."

—B. FRANKLIN SKINNER,
RETIRED CHAIRMAN & CEO,
BELLSOUTH TELECOMMUNICATIONS, INC.

"The Turknetts are leaders in contemporary leadership development and organization performance. Their beliefs are an essential part of leadership development at Pearl Izumi, and we will provide a copy of this book to managers/leaders in the company."

—JERRY EDWARDS, PRESIDENT, PEARL IZUMI

"The Turknetts impart a practical and actionable sense of how core values can be applied in the daily execution of business. I have personally benefited from many of their observations."

—GITHESH RAMAMURTHY,
CHAIRMAN & CEO, CCC INFORMATION SERVICES

"Character, respect, and responsibility are what we all need from our leaders today. As you read this book, you will see the applications to your business as well as your personal life."

—RUSS UMPHENOUR, CEO, RTM RESTAURANT GROUP, INC.

DECENT PEOPLE, DECENT COMPANY

DECENT
PEOPLE
DECENT
COMPANY

How to Lead with Character
at Work and in Life

ROBERT L. TURKNETT
CAROLYN N. TURKNETT

Davies-Black Publishing
Mountain View, California

RGQOOJ W

2 4 cm

207p.

To Rob, Josh, Jenny, and Jules

Published by Davies-Black Publishing, a division of CPP, Inc., 1055 Joaquin Road, Suite 200, Mountain View, CA 94043; 800-624-1765.

Special discounts on bulk quantities of Davies-Black books are available to corporations, professional associations, and other organizations. For details, contact the Director of Marketing and Sales at Davies-Black Publishing; 650-691-9123; fax 650-623-9271.

Visit the Davies-Black Publishing Web site at www.daviesblack.com.

09 08 07 06 05 10 9 8 7 6 5 4 3 2 1
Printed in the United States of America

Library of Congress Cataloging-in-Publication Data
Turknett, Robert L.
    Decent people, decent company : how to lead with character at work and in life / Robert L. Turknett & Carolyn N. Turknett—1st ed.
        p. cm.
    Includes bibliographical references and index.
    ISBN 0-89106-206-8 (hardcover)
    1. Leadership—Psychological aspects. 2. Organizational behavior. 3. Integrity. 4. Attitude (Psychology). 5. Emotional intelligence. 6. Quality of work life. I. Turknett, Carolyn N. II. Title.
HD57.7.T87 2005
658.4'092'019—dc22

2004018756

FIRST EDITION
First printing 2005

Contents

Foreword

After reading *Decent People, Decent Company,* one can't help but speculate on the dramatic impact it could have on the careers of so many businesspeople.

Few of us take the time for meaningful self-evaluation, identifying our areas of strength and those in which we could improve. This book is filled with examples of people who have done just that. Their rewards have been substantial.

Building on their experience in the private practice of psychology as well as their extensive experience in corporate leadership, Bob and Lyn Turknett offer here a highly readable and instructive lesson on how to create positive leadership at every organizational level. From learning the value of listening, to developing empathy, to demonstrating a belief in the value of every individual, they provide tools that can augment and accelerate the movement toward organizational—and personal—goals and objectives.

This book gives advice that works equally well for all employees. It examines core values that can be translated into more productive and satisfying personal interactions in the workplace. How do we encourage trust? Why is transparency important? What is the role of integrity even in the little things? How do we create an environment that allows for freedom of expression, disagreements, and even challenges to the propriety of proposed actions?

In my forty-three years at United Parcel Service, we grew to understand that the seeds of trust, respect, service excellence, and personal responsibility must be sown at all levels. We also grew to understand that those seeds required constant tending and nurturing in order to thrive. The Turknetts tell us the same is true of any company's core values. Without constant care, they will wither and die. This book offers all employees in every organization the opportunity to meet their responsibility to be effective leaders.

Kent C. "Oz" Nelson, former Chairman & CEO, UPS

Preface

We have worked together as a husband-and-wife team for more than twenty years, blending our disciplines of psychology and sociology to build a professional practice devoted to creating leadership at all levels. Our goal is to help people grow.

We have always believed that integrity and character are at the heart of good leadership. Based on our research and experience, we created the Leadership Character Model, which is at the heart of this book and guides our work. We picture the model as a scale, with *respect* and *responsibility* balancing on a base of *integrity.*

Developing the character for leadership is not an easy journey; we are still on the road ourselves. In this book, you'll see that when leaders build character, they foster organizational cultures that encourage decency and growth in everyone. Both the individual and the company win. So does society as a whole. Strengthening your Leadership Character is important whether you are

- A top leader who wants to make your company a place where everyone works as enthusiastically as you do

- A midmanager or team member who wants to lead more effectively and make a real difference

- An individual who wants to exercise creative leadership in your church or synagogue, neighborhood or city, or family

We were refining our ideas of Leadership Character (and working on this book) long before the breathtaking scandals at certain American companies came to light. Suddenly, the decency and values that should form every company's rock-solid foundation seem as hard to grasp as sand. The headiest economic boom in history has dissolved to reveal a shocking poverty of corporate ethics and leadership.

We admire American business and the effort and dedication so many people bring to their work. By and large, the companies and individuals we have worked with have tried hard to lead with integrity, but we should all be frightened by the pervasiveness of the corrosive cultures at Enron, WorldCom, and HealthSouth. Surely the leadership there failed miserably and should be held accountable, but none of us should sit back and say, "Look how bad they are." We all need to look inside. The transformation of organizations and individuals must be deeper and all-embracing. We're all participants, and it's up to each one of us to change how we think and behave.

When people are asked to list great leaders, names like Lincoln, Churchill, and Mandela are most often mentioned—people who were called to lead during times of war and social upheaval. These statesmen had already developed Leadership Character when they met the challenge. We believe this kind of character is necessary for every successful leader. In fact, it's the kind of character we all need.

Failures of leadership notwithstanding, we are optimistic. We believe this may be the *best* time for all of us to find the character and courage to lead. The crises we are facing today are perfect crucibles to shape leadership in all of us, and greatness in some.

The best leaders have confidence in themselves and respect for others. They have a sense of ownership of and responsibility for their entire organization, not just their own projects and work units. They know that by acting with integrity and vision, they can inspire those same values in everyone around them. They make the world a better place.

Explore with us how to become one of them.

Bob Turknett   *Lyn Turknett*
Robert L. Turknett, Ed.D.   *Carolyn N. Turknett, M.A.*

Acknowledgments

When you've lived for a relatively long time, one thing becomes clear: it's impossible to thank all the people who've contributed to your ideas. We are both in that boat. We owe a great debt to a great number of people.

Our largest debt for this book is owed to the clients we've been privileged to serve over the past twenty years. We've learned a lot from every individual and every company we've worked with. We are especially grateful to all those who agreed to be interviewed for this book. Their stories are the most meaningful part of the book.

We've also learned from our colleagues, particularly the talented people who have worked with us over the years at Turknett Leadership Group. We've gained so much from our long association—and long conversations—with Steve O'Brien, Michael Sessions, Barbara Reilly, and Karl Kuhnert. And two people on our staff, Suzanne LaVoy and Susan Hitchcock, deserve special thanks for the particular support they've given us on the book project and on the final manuscript.

We are also indebted to many, many friends and colleagues in our professional community. We've received unflagging support from Hagberg Consulting Group, a firm with whom we've worked closely for more than fifteen years.

We would never have finished this book without the able help of Robyn Spizman, Ron Laistch, and the amazingly gifted Jonathan Lerner. The staff members at Davies-Black were excellent guides through the editing process; Connie Kallback is surely the most helpful, affirming, and talented editor anywhere.

We are who we are because of our families. Our parents taught us about commitment, responsibility, love, and faith. Our two sons know us better than anyone and have been invaluable in the writing process—nixing some ideas, rewriting others, and generally keeping us honest.

And, finally, a special additional thank-you to Susan Hitchcock, who has been a colleague, a friend, and a model of leadership character for us.

About the Authors

Bob and Lyn Turknett have been (married) life partners for thirty-five years and business partners for twenty-five. They have lived in Atlanta, where they raised their sons, Rob and Josh, for more than twenty-five years. Previously in private practice, in 1987 they cofounded the Turknett Leadership Group, bringing their complementary disciplines and personalities together to better leverage their combined skills and to have a more overarching impact by concentrating on leadership development at all levels of organizations. Their joint passion is creating cohesive management teams that can build commitment, adapt to rapid change, and lead organizations to success. Stories of their work together are at the heart of this book

Lyn received her B.S. degree in mathematics and her M.A. degree in sociology, with special emphasis in organizational sociology, from the University of Georgia. Her main focus is on organization assessment and change, executive team development, and ethical leadership in rapidly changing environments. Bob received his undergraduate degree in business from Jacksonville University and his Ph.D. degree in psychology from the University of Georgia. He specializes in CEO consulting, executive team development, and individual development and coaching, and has served as an executive coach to hundreds of senior leaders in large and small businesses in a variety of industries.

Turknett Leadership Group serves clients of all sizes, from small entrepreneurial enterprises to large corporations, in a wide range of industries. Among its clients are AGL Resources, American Cancer Society, BellSouth, Bennett International Group, CNL Restaurant Properties, Inc., Elekta, Federal Home Loan Bank of Atlanta, Freebairn & Co., Georgia-Pacific Corporation, Hewlett-Packard, Kodak, MATRIX Resources, Mercer Human Resources Consulting, RTM Restaurant Group, and XcelleNet.

———

Being a good corporate citizen is important to Bob and Lyn. Both are avid volunteers for the United Way of Metropolitan Atlanta and have served in various leadership capacities. They currently chair the Johnnetta B. Cole Society for Leadership Giving, and each year they donate both their own time and that of their staff to pro bono work.

Introduction

We believe that the foundation of leadership must be character, and that the foundation of leadership character must be integrity. Without an underpinning of integrity, leadership ultimately fails. Leaders' mistakes, even enormous ones, can be overcome. But failures of integrity cannot.

American culture is largely shaped by business. Business leaders, occupying positions of power, have a huge impact on the culture, which gives them both opportunities and obligations. We want to influence them to exercise their leadership from a foundation of integrity.

"There are two arguments for treating people decently," an article in the *Financial Times* recently argued. "The first is that it is right, and the second is that it is profitable. [But] it says something about the moral environment that most advocates of treating workers decently feel obliged to rely on the second argument rather than the first."[1]

We agree that when companies create trust, treat everyone with respect, and encourage leadership at every level they are tremendously more successful. We've seen this over and over. But we also firmly believe that companies and individuals have a moral imperative to behave with integrity, whether it leads to financial success or not.

The idea that the sole goal of a public company is to increase shareholder value is deficient—and unsustainable. Pursuit of shareholder value without respect to employees and customers, community and environment, demeans our collective humanity. It impoverishes our world, both literally and spiritually. People and companies with character do not think that way.

Most of the businesspeople we know strive to conduct themselves with integrity. But some fail. The corrosive culture of selfishness that took hold at Enron, for example, obscured ethical concerns and the good of the organization. The culture celebrated mavericks who were smart and answerable to no one. It was precisely the mistaken notion that talented individuals could be freed from responsibility to the organization as a whole and to the larger community—and freed from conforming to codes of ethical conduct—that helped create Enron's implosion.

MODELS OF INTEGRITY AND CHARACTER

"I am not a hero. I just did what
any decent person would have done."

The speaker was Miep Gies, a secretary in a Dutch chemicals business. Gies considered herself an ordinary person, but she had extraordinary integrity. Her Jewish employer, Otto Frank, with his family and four other Jews, tried to escape the Nazi roundups by moving into a secret apartment on the company's premises. Gies provided food and protection. When the fugitives were discovered and sent to concentration camps, she defied Nazi orders and returned to the apartment. Scattered across the floor were the handwritten pages of the now-famous diary kept by Frank's daughter Anne. Gies gathered the pages and saved them. As a result of her simple acts of bravery, the world was enriched with a literary work of extraordinary humanity and moral power.

Gies's comment modestly states that what she did was nothing special. Yet it took incredible courage for her to remain true to her values—for instance, the value of respect for others regardless of their heritage—and to translate those values into action. This is character, and any decent person must have it. "It's easy enough to state your values and personal integrity during the good times," says Bill George, author of *Authentic Leadership*, "but what really counts is how you perform under extreme pressure. That's when the character and value of a person are determined. It is during this time that you establish your moral compass—a sense of right and wrong."[2] Miep Gies lived with integrity while risking arrest and death. When our everyday circumstances are so much less dire, how can we not do the same?

Think of the most inspiring people you have worked with. What are the qualities that set them apart? Aren't they the brave ones who stand up for what they believe? Can't they always be counted on to tell the truth—and not to twist facts or "work the system" for personal advantage? Can't they also be counted on to follow through on commitments—to do what they say they will do, when they say they'll do it?

These are people with integrity. Whatever their job titles may be, they are the ones who move things forward, inspire commitment from colleagues, keep the group on course—and are willing to question that course when necessary, too. These are the real leaders, who generate and sustain cultures of character in their organizations. Every one of us is capable of developing the core qualities of leadership character and becoming one of them.

Top leaders may bear the greatest responsibility for establishing a culture of character within an organization. But if we just leave it to CEOs and board members to behave respectfully and responsibly, we will not get very far. If you don't think you're contributing anything of value to the company you work for, and you can't figure out how to do so, why are you accepting a paycheck? Do something proactive or move on. Solve the problems you see. Anyone can sit on the bench and complain, but no one deserves to be paid for it.

——

We're talking about taking responsibility for what you think is wrong or could be improved—whether it's an ethical lapse you see, an opportunity for developing a new product, a nonsensical process that needs correcting, or a promotion you think you deserve—and doing so in a way that works and that encourages others to join you in the effort.

Creating a culture of character requires hard work every day by every member of an organization. It requires that each of us believe that part of our purpose on this earth is to become better people. It means embracing the paradox that because we are fallible—unable to be truly perfect, or to perfect anything—the potential for growth never ceases. It means taking individual responsibility for every family, team, community, or organization we belong to. And that means taking responsibility not only for the successes of those enterprises, such as growth and profits, but also for their ethics and daily conduct.

We believe that developing character and integrity can be the most rewarding thing you've ever done. It allows you to accomplish more; to genuinely like your job more; to commit more fully to whatever you're doing, whether that's running a Fortune 500 company, organizing a PTA fundraiser, or managing a major project at work; and to simply enjoy yourself more as you interact with others. It allows you to lead in a way that lends integrity to everything you touch.

RESPONSIBILITY, RESPECT, AND A FOUNDATION OF INTEGRITY

When we say individuals have character, we first mean that they are decent, honest, authentic human beings: they have integrity. We also mean they work hard and get results: they're responsible. And we recognize that they treat other people with respect and the belief that they're equally important. Responsibility and respect are the two essential components of leadership character; integrity is its grounding.

———

Companies with character are just like people with character. They get results, but they do it with integrity—responsibly and respectfully. Like people of character, companies of character are able to balance the core qualities of responsibility, such as accountability and courage, with the core qualities of respect, such as humility and lack of blame.

In this book, we share what we have learned about how people and organizations can develop these core qualities and build their leadership character. We've seen how much happier people are, whatever their job, when they take responsibility not just for their careers, but for who they are and for the organizations they are in. Wherever you are, you can be more effective at getting things done, solving problems, and making things happen if you are willing to think more about what needs to be done than about what's wrong with other people. If you act in the best interest of the organization you're a part of, you'll find that things go better for the organization and for you. Our model is designed to help individuals learn how to lead by understanding the essential aspects of true leadership character.

Central to our understanding is the simple but powerful knowledge that the individual and the organization are not separate in how they behave or in how they grow. If you lead with character, wherever you are in the hierarchy, you can help create an organization in which

- All participants are aware of their contributions and willing to challenge the ethics of any action

- Everyone takes responsibility for and ownership of success

- All members treat each other with decency and respect, feel they all have a seat at the table, and want to enthusiastically invest their energies

We have spent most of our career working with senior leaders, helping them develop these qualities. We are passionate about this work because we know that through it we have made a difference in the lives of many, many others. We have great admiration for the leaders we have worked with, many of whom you will hear from in this book. Most of these individuals are—and already were, before we met them—excellent leaders. They worked hard to open themselves to change. Most of them would now agree that character development can and should continue throughout a lifetime. There is no one who cannot deepen his or her character. If each of us embraces that idea, our organizations and our society will be stronger and healthier.

You can approach the character challenge from either place— that is, as an individual who wants to grow your own leadership, or as a member who wants to grow your organization's character. This book will help you focus on and develop your own core qualities of character; and by doing that, you will inevitably become a force for the growth of integrity and character throughout your organization. Our fervent hope is that you will take what we offer and use it to make a positive difference in the world.

PART ONE

INTEGRITY— THE NATURE OF CHARACTER

1

Character, Culture, and Change

E arly in his career, Bob was the psychologist for the Brevard County school system in Florida. As part of his job, he routinely visited all the schools in the county, and afterward he would come home and talk about what he'd seen: "Different schools have such different feels," he said. "At some, the kids all seem so happy. They have their work and drawings posted everywhere, but the rooms feel orderly. The teachers seem to love their jobs. And I don't know how they do it, but the principals seem to know every kid's name. The kids love to see their principal coming down the hall. But at other schools nobody seems happy. The teachers sound like they're yelling and pleading all the time. I've heard some really harsh words, and you hardly see the principal outside the office. Some schools are just so chaotic I can't see how anybody's learning a thing."

Each school had its own personality or culture. Bob soon realized the difference was due in large part to the type of leadership coming from the principal. Where the school's personality was negative, the principal was often remote and rigid; there were lots of unnecessary rules, and the teachers felt micromanaged. Where there was an absence of discipline the principal tended to be permissive and ineffectual. Where there was a positive atmosphere the principal was visible and engaged and seemed to encourage creativity and new ideas from both teachers and students. Most other factors were equal. It was one school system with uniform rules and guidelines, and ostensibly the same high standards in all schools. Most of the neighborhoods had similar demographics. But different styles of leadership produced different results because organizations are malleable. Performance tended to be higher in schools with positive personalities. In every case, the leadership emanating from the principal made a significant difference between a happy school and a hostile one, a good place to learn and a poor one. Each school was a distinct social system affected by the specific inputs of the leadership it received.

The leadership of any organization plays a primary role in creating its culture. Bob's observations in the schools bear that out. It's also true that the nominal leaders don't do it alone. In all social systems every participant makes a contribution, whether actively or passively, intentionally or unconsciously, creatively or destructively. Power doesn't flow only from the top to the bottom; people at every level of an organization have influence on its tenor, style, and ultimate effectiveness. Human beings are also malleable, and so are social systems such as corporations and workplaces. How we think of ourselves affects the nature of our participation and, in turn, the culture of the organization itself.

LEADERSHIP CAN COME FROM ANYONE
The Customer Care Club

At a supermarket in a small town in Georgia, an assistant manager had initiated a "customer care team" for employees, but two weeks later he was promoted and transferred to another location. Alice, the assistant front-end manager, and Oscar, the produce manager, had been excited about the project and couldn't stand the thought of letting it go. They went to Gordon, the store's general manager, for permission to continue the project. "Ideas were just popping in our heads," Alice recalls. "We chose the name customer care club instead of team because some people saw *team* as something management sets up. But *club* seemed to mean that others who want to can join. We thought that if we increased employee morale, it would increase customer satisfaction."

They decided to start with the break room. It was a mess: small and dingy with a seven-foot ceiling that made it seem like a cell, and an old microwave with a broken latch. They couldn't make the room bigger, but they could make it better and brighter. They painted the room themselves, and Alice had the idea of painting a blue sky and clouds on the ceiling. Management agreed to install a new microwave and a snack machine, which might not sound like much of a victory in a food store but actually took the club members' best powers of persuasion.

Then, an employee newsletter was started. "It's always good to see your name in the newspaper," Alice explains, "and the paper helps us recognize even the little things members do to serve customers better."

"Employees are excited: They look at their newsletters before they look at their paychecks," Gordon says. "Another way we give recognition is to bring members into the weekly department head meeting and talk about the special things they've done for customers."

"We also realized that we needed input from our customers," adds Oscar, who built and installed a writing shelf under the store bulletin board to hold comment cards and pens. The store responds to all complaints, but now most comments are positive. "Members now seem to care about what happens to the store," Oscar says. "They don't just do one job—they take care of the whole store. Before, when you'd ask people to do something other than their exact job responsibilities, they would say, 'I don't get paid to do that.' Now, they come in to work smiling and do what needs to be done. Turnover is decreasing, and teens are telling their friends that this is a good place to work."

Gordon has been confident enough in his skills as a manager to let employees not only take the lead but also give him feedback on his management style. "Originally I was a hatchet man, but I've mellowed over the years; I've learned to listen more. Before, I'd sometimes go out just to walk around the store, but at times I'd have something else on my mind and I wouldn't speak to anyone. I heard about a teenage employee who thought I didn't like her because I ignored her. That was a lesson for me."

Everyone reports that Gordon's leadership style has changed dramatically, and he agrees. "I always allowed only department heads to give me feedback in closed management meetings," Gordon says. "Now, though, everyone can tell me what they think, and they can do it throughout the day." It has paid off for him in reduced stress. "I used to worry. Now when I leave the store, I know I have fifteen or twenty people I can count on to have my interest and the store's interests at heart."

"Results have been excellent," he concludes. "There's been a reduction in the number of negative comments, an increase in production in the store, an increase in the number of customer compliments, an increase in positive 1-800 calls, and—best of all— a double-digit increase in sales."

• • •

RELATIONAL LEADERSHIP

Clearly, we can change our minds about leadership. For example, we can decide that leadership is something we each participate in and can contribute to no matter where we are in the hierarchy. Changing our minds changes the way we behave, and that makes possible changes in other people and in the very system in which we are operating.

In a 1996 article, William Drath, a research scientist at the Center for Creative Leadership, wrote:

> *There are leaders, but they don't make leadership happen. And there are followers, but they are not the objects of the leader's leadership behavior. Leaders and followers alike participate in leadership. Leadership is a property of the relationships people form when they are doing something together. Good sets of relationships constitute good leadership, which produces good leaders and good followers.*[1]

Leadership, in other words, is an aspect and function of a social system, not just of particular individuals within it, and everyone who participates in the system has the responsibility to contribute to it.

Organizations must be understood and structured in ways that encourage this kind of participation. The information age technologies we all now work with have made this change both imperative and inevitable as they enable virtually instant communication and networking among people at all levels, inside and outside an organization. The old up-and-down-only dynamic has been replaced. Of course, some positions still entail more power and responsibility than others, but we all know that managing in today's environment is not about issuing orders and imposing control. It's about awareness, resilience, and adaptation; about listening, coaching, collaborating, and evolving. Those qualities are only possible when everyone feels responsible for the enterprise as a whole, respectful *of* it and respected *by* it as well.

We Create the Systems We Are In

What you believe about yourself and others, about how organizations work, and about leadership and hierarchies has an enormous impact on what you see and experience as you participate in an organization. Many organizational theorists believe that social reality and social behavior are not preprogrammed but rather dynamically created by the people involved. This idea, called *social constructivism,* holds that our ideas about how that reality is created affect what we create.

Whether it's objectively true or not, if you believe that the company for which you work does not want your input, you probably will keep your ideas to yourself and eventually will come to feel degraded and resentful. Your experience of the organization will be a negative one.

This could be your experience even if the organization is not so rigidly hierarchical. The top-down models we all have in our heads from early learning can make us behave as though it's true, even when no one, including top leadership, consciously wants it that way. What happens is people don't try things; they box themselves in; they sit down and shut up (or just complain at the water cooler) when they could make a difference if they tried. Even top leaders who proclaim they want people in the organization to take initiative may at times reflexively fall back into the old style, too, thinking, "I'm in charge here," and fail to listen.

If, instead, you believe your ideas are good ones and your colleagues should hear them, you're more likely to express yourself freely and to have a more powerful experience of participation.

The work of David Cooperrider, professor of organizational behavior at Case Western Reserve University, and his colleagues grew out of this kind of thinking. Called *Appreciative Inquiry,* it is grounded in social constructivism theory, the idea that we create social reality as we go, cocreating it continually with those around us.

Cooperrider believes the attitudes we have toward an organization and the assumptions we bring to the situation will have a profound impact on what we find and experience there. If a change agent, such as an outside consultant or senior leader new to the enterprise, approaches an organization seeing it as nothing more than a collection of problems to be figured out and solved, the people within the organization will come to see the company that way and become more and more dispirited. If the change agent, however, starts by looking for what is going right and assumes there are existing strengths to find, people within the organization develop energy, enthusiasm, and an appreciation of the strengths of the whole. Cooperrider has written:

> *Organizations are products of human interaction and mind rather than some blind expression of an underlying natural order. Deceptively simple yet so entirely radical in implication, this insight is still shattering many beliefs, one of which is the long-standing conviction that bureaucracy, oligarchy, and other forms of hierarchical domination are inevitable. Today we know that this simply is not true.*[2]

Another belief this notion shatters is that people who do not happen to be placed high in the power structure lack the ability to exert influence on the whole.

We ourselves are not by any means strict social constructivists. We don't think, for instance, that a tyrannical boss would necessarily be any more benevolent just because his underlings were somehow convinced to see him that way. We do think there's a good deal of truth in the idea that we have considerable power over our experience of reality. The top leaders within any organization are the primary originators of its culture, but any member is capable of having an influence over it, too. (Our study of organizational behavior has led us to believe that balanced views are usually best. When theories compete, there are often important truths to be gleaned from many visions.)

As we have said, the views people have about themselves and others, and about the way the organization works, make a huge difference in what they see and how they behave. We create our reality. If leaders have an especially big impact on that reality, it's primarily because everyone else pays so much attention to their ideas, behaviors, and moods.

Cooperrider believes those of us serving as agents of change should take an "appreciative" approach, building on the positives we find, to help the organization actually become more positive and healthier. This central theme of Appreciative Inquiry is of great value to us in our work. We encourage you to try it yourself.

We Get What We Expect

In his first inaugural address, Abraham Lincoln called on his fellow Americans to summon "the better angels of our nature." Summoning our nobler side—the part that doesn't take the easy way out, that makes the decent choice even when it's difficult; that forgives; that doesn't take advantage of others—usually takes a conscious decision and some effort, but it's well worth it. People who consciously try to bring out the best in themselves and others are happier and more successful because the effort usually works. To some degree at least, we end up seeing what we are looking for.

Lyn was an avid gardener when our children were young. "One year," she remembers, "I saved the seeds from a particularly delicious cantaloupe. The next spring I planted them. The vines grew really vigorously and started flowering. Fruit began forming, but it kept turning dark. I figured something was wrong with them, and I kept throwing these 'rotten cantaloupes' away. Then one day our oldest son, Rob, who was five at the time, came in from the garden. He said, 'Mom, it's so funny—your cantaloupes look just like that squash we once had for supper.' The seeds, of course, were not from a cantaloupe vine but from an acorn squash; I'd mixed them up. And because I was looking for something else, I had thrown away a lot of perfectly good squash!"

If We Expect Better, We Get That, Too

Expectations work the same way in organizations. The way managers and leaders view the people they are managing makes a remarkable difference in their subordinates' behavior and performance. If a manager acts with the belief that a direct report is not very capable, that employee is likely to demonstrate mediocre behavior. If a manager believes the best about a worker's capabilities, good work is the more probable result.

In a 1977 study, male college students were shown pictures of several women and asked to rate them as attractive or unattractive.[3] Then each student had a telephone conversation with one of the women. Before the call was made, the student was given a picture of one of the previously rated women and told that she was the person with whom he was speaking. After the phone "date," the student was asked for his impressions. As expected, when he thought he was talking to an attractive woman, he rated her as warmer and friendlier. More startling was the next phase of the experiment. Independent observers were asked to listen in on the phone conversations and then give their impressions of the women. The women who were talking to men who *thought* they were attractive were rated by the observers as warmer and friendlier, even though they had seen no pictures. The callers actually seemed to elicit the behavior they were expecting. This phenomenon has been called *behavioral confirmation;* it seems that our expectations about behavior are powerful enough to elicit that very behavior.

In another famous experiment, Robert Rosenthal, a professor of social psychology at Harvard University, and his colleague, Lenore Jacobson, worked with elementary school children from eighteen classrooms.[4] They chose 20 percent of the children at random from each room and told their teachers that they were "intellectual bloomers." They explained that these children could be expected to show remarkable gains during the school year. Indeed, the students in the designated group showed average IQ gains of two points in verbal ability, seven points in reasoning, and four points in overall IQ. They really did bloom because their teachers expected them to.

Such studies have been repeated many times with business managers and show that leaders can change the performance of those who report to them by changing the way they think about those employees.

This isn't magic, and it isn't really even mysterious. Like the expectations of the men about the women in the telephone experiment, and of the schoolteachers about the supposedly gifted children, the beliefs of managers about their workers can translate into all kinds of subtle but tangible behaviors that help produce precisely the expected results. From observation, the speculation is that these results are caused by subtle changes in behavior, particularly nonverbal behavior. When teachers believe students are gifted, they tend to look at them more, smile at them more, stand closer to their desks, and offer them more encouragement. Similarly, a manager who is confident that a direct report can do a good job may be more likely to offer help getting past obstacles without becoming impatient; to supply needed resources; and even to make offhand supportive remarks. But a manager who expects someone to fail at a task is likely to react to problems with irritation, convey pessimism through body language and tone of voice, and even withhold resources with the unconscious idea that they would just be wasted.

Expectation, Attitude, and the Bottom Line

In his classic 1960 book, *The Human Side of Enterprise*, Douglas McGregor formulated two models of managerial attitude called Theory X and Theory Y. Theory X managers, who assume that people are basically unwilling to work and need to be cajoled and directed, rarely get from their staffs the level of performance, participation, and interest Theory Y managers get. Is it any wonder? Theory Y managers assume that work is as natural as play, that people work hard for organizations to whose aims they are committed, and that they naturally seek to take responsibility.

Recent work on emotional intelligence in leadership gives us good clues as to why Theory Y leaders succeed. Leaders who can elicit and drive emotions in a positive way create more positive work climates. Daniel Goleman, the author of *Emotional Intelligence* and *Primal Leadership*, calls them "resonant" leaders. Their mind-set is, "We're all committed to the same goals, and all willing to work hard to achieve them." They are operating from a place of respect, imbuing the culture of their workplace with a sense of worth and thus having a resonating effect on everyone else there. We'll discuss this further in the chapter on empathy, as it is empathy that enables these leaders to have such a positive effect.

Positive leadership has value far beyond the relative pleasantness of the office or store where some people are obligated to spend their days. One study assessed CEOs and their management teams on how upbeat (energetic, enthusiastic, optimistic, and determined) they were.[5] It found that the more positive the overall mood in the top team was and the better the team worked together, the better the company's business results. The study also examined the effects of personality clashes and friction in meetings. The finding? The longer a company was run by a management team that did not get along internally, the poorer that company's market return was. Goleman also reports on a study of thirty-two stores in a retail chain, showing that the outlets with the most positive salespeople had the best sales results and confirming that the culture of positive attitude was set from the top, by the manager of each store.[6]

SELF-EFFICACY: BELIEVING IN YOURSELF

One of the goals of the Leadership Character Model is to encourage people to develop what behavioral theorists call *self-efficacy*. People with self-efficacy view themselves as able to control their environments and effect change. They are resilient and hardy. Like everyone else, they face challenges, but their optimism and belief in themselves enable them to respond positively. They don't see themselves as victims, and they don't see their successes as the result of luck. Put another way, people who get things done believe in themselves.

Research indicates that people who have a sense of commitment, involvement, and engagement with others, and who see themselves as able to control things around them, tend to respond more positively to changes in their work environment.[7] Two people can be in the same situation, but the one with low self-efficacy will see it as a situation he can't control or do anything about so he may not even try, while the person with high self-efficacy will assume she can do something, go ahead and try, and frequently succeed. Those with high self-efficacy experience less stress and report that their work is more enjoyable. Such hardiness may come naturally to some of us, while others may need to work on developing it, but hardiness is an attitude. It's a way of framing your relationship to your environment positively, and it can be enormously empowering. Just consider the difference between saying, after a proposal you made has been rejected, "I guess I'm not the person who should try to solve this problem," and "What can I think of to make my next proposal work?"

In his 1996 book *Leadership IQ*, Emmett Murphy reported on a study of 18,000 leaders in 562 companies.[8] People at all levels were asked to nominate the most effective leaders, and through this process, a sample of 1,029 exceptional leaders was identified. Murphy called these individuals *workleaders* because he believes that real leaders really work. Murphy found that, compared to a group of 1,000 average leaders who were selected randomly from the same organizations, the workleaders scored higher by 28 percent in sales volume, 35 percent in profit margins, 71 percent in customer satisfaction, and 53 percent in customer retention.

Murphy's most fascinating findings were about the attitudes of the workleaders. The 1,029 workleaders were asked to rank the factors that had contributed most to their success. Their rankings were then compared to the self-rankings of the group of 1,000 randomly selected leaders.

The workleaders saw aspects of their self-efficacy as crucial to their personal success: their experience on the front lines, their taking of full responsibility for the enterprise, and their willingness to go first to make things happen. They also saw gaining the respect of colleagues and customers as very important. Luck was last on the list. Average leaders, on the other hand, saw their success as dependent on external forces and other people, like support from the organization or the boss, and luck.

Real leaders think they can accomplish things. They don't say "I can't get anything done because the leaders of this organization don't walk the talk, my boss doesn't know what she's doing, and nobody gives me any direction." There can be times when such statements truly describe an organization, and times when you really do need to move on to a better situation. But real leaders don't focus on negative feelings like those. If you focus on what's wrong, it blinds you to the good in the situation and to your own capabilities to make it better. A positive attitude engenders hardiness, and hardiness promotes success.

POWER WORKS FROM THE BOTTOM UP, AND FROM SIDE TO SIDE

Gwen's Story

Just as leaders in a company can change the people who work for them through the attitudes and expectations they display, people at other levels can change their superiors and colleagues.

Gwen is an IT executive with high potential, an intelligent, eager learner, passionately focused on helping her company succeed. In her first consultation, she reported a very negative relationship with Beth, an executive peer. They were constantly at odds. Bob suggested that for two weeks Gwen make a conscious effort to change how she acted and reacted toward her co-worker. He suggested that she not be negative toward Beth, verbally or nonverbally; that she make a point of complimenting her for jobs well done; and that in general she make only positive comments to her as long as they were based on fact.

"In a coaching session," Bob says, "I told her how I had once recommended this approach years earlier to a sales manager who had an awful relationship with his boss. The boss really was down on him, but this sales manager didn't realize that through nonverbal behavior, avoidance, and offhand comments he was giving back the same message that the boss wasn't doing his own job well either. Getting Dave to deliberately use positive behavior for just two weeks changed that entire relationship, and the way they viewed each other."

Gwen could see the theoretical benefit of displaying only positive behavior toward her colleague, but at first, because of the anger and resentment she had built up toward this person, she was just not motivated to do it. Gwen felt that she had been treated rudely, and that now the colleague did not "deserve" for her to be nice. At this stage, Gwen lacked *emotional mastery,* which we will discuss in depth in chapter 4. We had to first help her recognize her anger and reframe the thoughts that caused her to feel it. As Gwen's situation showed, resolving problems with another person almost always involves two steps: changing your emotional reactions to the person, and then changing your actions toward the person.

We helped Gwen replace her angry, blaming thoughts with ideas more like, "Instead of telling myself this situation is awful and wasting energy feeling angry, I will recognize that it is merely unfortunate and direct my energies toward solving the problem." Then she was able to try being deliberately positive in the relationship, and it worked. Her relationship with her colleague began to improve.

But Gwen was most excited when she urged a friend to use what she had learned. The friend, who worked in another department, was ready to quit because she had such a horrible relationship with her boss. She told Gwen that her boss ignored her, never coached her, criticized her gratuitously, and showed favoritism to others. Gwen convinced her to try this technique of maintaining a positive attitude for two weeks. Within a single week that relationship began to change, and within three the friend was amazed to report to Gwen how helpful, complimentary, and positive her boss had become.

When Gwen realized her relationship with her colleague was transformed, she became animated. She seemed more engaged in her work and her company. Similarly, when she told of her friend's success with her boss, it was easy to see that this had "made Gwen's day." When people start to behave in ways consistent with good Leadership Character, as Gwen did, it is always a *win-win outcome.* The individuals experience a heightened sense of effectiveness and well-being, and the organization reaps the benefit of that enthusiasm and motivation.

Gwen's experience also demonstrates how effective peer coaching can be, once a person understands how to make these changes in attitude and action. In sharing the story of how she had been able to reframe her thinking and then build a strong relationship with her colleague, Gwen motivated her friend to do the same. Even if Gwen had not succeeded in either case—with her colleague or with influencing her friend—she still would have been modeling good Leadership Character. Her successes, however, are self-reinforcing, and they make it likely that she will continue using these attitudes and actions in solving her own problems as well as in helping others learn and use these approaches.

Gwen and her friend were able to bring about change in people they worked with because of two things. Even though they were not in positions of power over the people with whom they were experiencing conflict, the organizational social system responded to their input, as it always will. And their willingness to change their own behavior first was crucial. They were willing to grow.

• • •

CREATING VIBRANT CULTURES
Chuck's Story

We first met Chuck Johnson in the early 1980s. He lived in our neighborhood, and he and Bob became tennis buddies. A few years later, we transitioned from primarily private practice to management psychology and organizational consulting. (We were working then with Rich Hagberg, Ph.D., a consulting psychologist from California, one of the first to do executive assessment and coaching. We still use the tools he created and continues to develop.) By this time, Chuck had a start-up firm, Sales Technologies. "We built Sales Technologies relatively quickly," Chuck remembers, "and hired some experienced senior people. Unlike a lot of early-stage technology companies that have a lot of young people, these folks had a fair amount of real, large-company experience. Still, the challenge for us was to create one culture from many."

Chuck asked us to work with Sales Technologies, which involved doing everything from leadership assessment and coaching, to CEO consulting, to devising leadership training and action learning programs. But our first attention went to Chuck's top managers. "Once that team had established their working relationships," he says, "we needed help with the next level in the organization. There we did have some people who hadn't worked for a large company: brand-new managers, many times supervising brand-new employees, many of whom were just into their first jobs. All that can be a recipe for disaster, especially where the culture's still just coming about and you don't yet have any employee handbook you can reach for.

"Some of these folks were still young enough that the leadership development work made permanent changes in how they operated and behaved. By getting them to pay attention to how people interact within organizations, the organization development team created a mentality whereby folks would say, 'Let me just stop and think about this situation, and how do I best approach it. What tools have I learned? Why is this person different from me?'

"Companies succeed or fail because of management," observes Chuck. In his current work as managing partner of Noro-Moseley Partners, one of the largest and most experienced venture capital firms in the southeastern United States, Chuck has seen a lot of start-ups do both. "The difficulty is in building a team—an infrastructure—and knowing as a leader, for example, when you need to add people to complement yourself. Also, most younger companies don't realize the value of investing in developing people." When Chuck invests in start-ups now, he always insists that leadership development consulting be built in. "It's part of the due diligence," he says. "We owe it to our investors. Then, at the end of the day, if you get the right people and the right team and build an open, creative culture, you usually have a successful business."

• • •

SEEING YOURSELF AS DYNAMIC

Frances Hesselbein, former CEO of Girl Scouts of the USA, who now chairs the board of the Leader to Leader Institute (formerly the Peter F. Drucker Foundation for Nonprofit Management), says that "leadership is about how to be, not how to do."[9] Indeed, the first task of leaders is not to work on skill sets or techniques, but to work on who they are: on their character. When thinking about character development, we find it helpful to consider the Buddhist concept of *kokoro*. *Kokoro* can translate as both "mind" and "heart." It implies a dynamic, rather than static, idea of how to be, an ongoing process of perfecting one's character throughout the span of one's life. One Westerner observed this about *kokoro:* "Being is thought of as dynamic, something one does on purpose, not as an accident or automatically."

In our culture, we don't typically think of ourselves growing, learning, and developing character once we become adults. We tend to see ourselves as "grown up," as complete when we finish high school or college and enter the work world, or when we marry and start a family. It seems as if the only changes we expect consist of racking up awards and accomplishments: promotions and raises at work, or kids, or bigger houses. If you see yourself instead as dynamic and growing, and open to personal change, those awards and accomplishments are just as likely to come, but your life will be deeper, richer, and more satisfying.

The focus of this book is the workplace, but the principles discussed here apply to your whole life. In our consulting practice we also concentrate on helping people grow in the context of their work. In fact, your job is an ideal arena in which to make your Leadership Character unfold. Work is where you spend most of your adult life. It is the place where your best attention and highest creativity are demanded and rewarded. At work, you are part of a system, surrounded by people pursuing common goals.

Inevitably, work is also a place where you find yourself frustrated, at odds with others, and called upon sometimes to do tasks or to think in ways that do not come easily. As they were for Gwen and her friend, such challenges can be transformed into sources of growth, but the qualities you can develop in yourself by applying the Leadership Character Model will be just as useful to you when you organize a fund-raising campaign for an arts organization, or participate on a search committee at your church, or become an officer in your neighborhood association. You'll find that work is a great place to build your character, but the character you build there will serve you well wherever you are.

Key Concepts

- Leadership shapes an organization's culture, but power works from the bottom up, too; we all help create the systems we are in.

- We get what we expect. If we expect better, we get that, in ourselves, in others, and in our organizations.

- Self-efficacy is key: people who believe in themselves accomplish things.

- To lead for positive change, build on the positives: positive ideas of yourself and others, positive attitudes, and positive influences.

2

The Leadership Character Model

E d had developed a software program that enabled companies in the travel industry to save millions of dollars by changing how they sold space. He decided to use this product to start his own firm. Bright, energetic, inspiring, and likable, as CEO, Ed enjoyed the fast pace of starting a new business. What he did not enjoy so much was the actual day-to-day running of a company. He had a tendency to put off tedious tasks.

He soon realized that it was time to bring in a president to run the rapidly growing enterprise, someone with proven experience who enjoyed operations management. Marcus was the choice. He was a person driven to succeed in whatever he undertook, who took pleasure in making certain that every aspect of an operation was running smoothly. He also liked to run things his way.

Before long, conflict arose between Marcus and the CEO, much of which revolved around control issues. Ed very much wanted to be liked, and he treated people in a way that made it easy for them to like him. Marcus paid much more attention to getting things done than to the reactions of others. He was quick to tell Ed, in a direct way, how he thought things should be. He also thought Ed was too lax in holding others accountable. Ed's response was to avoid conflict with Marcus to try to buy time to figure out how to work with his aggressive and demanding behavior, but it only resulted in more procrastination on Ed's part. Marcus then became more frustrated and pushed harder, giving Ed the message that he was not being effective as the CEO. Ed did not feel Marcus respected him as his leader; rather, it seemed that Marcus was competing with him. Other members of the management team noticed this, too, and urged Ed to do something about it.

The relationship between the two top leaders was unproductive both for them and for the company. Other people's morale and productivity were affected. Marcus's demanding and controlling personality seemed at odds with the high-energy, creative atmosphere Ed had fostered from the beginning. The staff began to feel apprehensive about the young organization. Although the tense relationship between the two men had specific impacts on this company, dichotomies like this between leaders are not at all unusual. The problem? Leaders fail to see the need for personal balance within themselves. A true partnership, like true leadership, requires eliminating domination by the more assertive force through developing the skills of respect, and equally important, eliminating abdication by the more humanistic force through growing stronger in the skills of responsibility.

EVOLUTION OF THE MODEL

Many of us have been frustrated by difficult business relationships. We see problems that need correcting. We want better relationships with our colleagues and fewer obstacles to getting things done, but we don't know how to resolve these issues. What we need is a leadership tool that *real people* in the trenches can use to work through these frustrations to build better relationships.

The Leadership Character Model was designed to meet this need. The model isn't theoretical or confusing; it's accessible and practical. This model achieves several simple but crucial goals: It enables people to look at who they are and how they approach leadership, and it serves as an easy-to-use tool to help them accomplish the things they want to do.

The Leadership Character Model is depicted as a common scale, one you might see in a chemist's lab (Figure 1). The base of the scale is *integrity*. That's the incorruptible foundation authentic leadership must rest on. Integrity is essential to behaving with honesty, decency, and authenticity, but it is fluid, too. It's the product of a consciousness continually refreshed with the awareness that situations evolve and opposing forces must be reconciled. Your sense of integrity must keep growing to meet these challenges.

The platforms at the ends of the scale represent *respect* and *responsibility*, two key leadership qualities you must always strive to keep in balance on your foundation of integrity. *Respect* describes the sense of partnership, participation, and equality you want to feel in any organization or company you are involved in. It's the sense that although everyone may not be equal in terms of salary or position, each role is viewed as vital. As a leader, it's important

FIGURE 1: The Leadership Character Model

29

to be sure your subordinates see that in this company, people are treated as equals, and that *course corrections* are made without the need to assign blame. For you as the manager or as a team member, respect means being listened to and listening attentively to others. It comes from gaining control over your volatile emotions yet having the confidence to put forward your own skills and ideas—that is, demonstrating respect for yourself. Respect means loyalty even if you sometimes disagree, recognizing that some decisions must be made by others. The core qualities of respect, represented as weights on the respect platform, are *empathy, lack of blame, emotional mastery,* and *humility.*

Responsibility, the other side of the scale, means both dependability and full engagement. It involves the willingness to hold both yourself and others accountable with fairness and objectivity. When you are responsible, you're assertive, willing to take risks and accept the consequences of your actions. You see the day-to-day issues, yet you can envision the bigger picture, taking seriously the needs and successes of the organization as a whole, as if you were one of its owners. The core qualities of responsibility are *self-confidence, accountability, focus on the whole,* and *courage.*

INTEGRITY: PRECIOUS AND POWERFUL

A consistent reputation for integrity is difficult to build and very easy to undermine or destroy through careless behavior. That is especially true in the modern workplace, which can cause troubling problems for employers. Downturns in the business cycle such as the one that followed the dot-com bust may force employees to put up with jobs they don't love for a while, but ideas that would have seemed frivolous to our parents' generation are now widely assumed to be true: we have options in the world of work, we don't have to stick with people we don't trust, and above all there's no need to put up with coercive, abusive leadership. People no longer so willingly take orders when the orders don't make sense to them or the person in command seems unworthy of that role. Leadership today is not as much about commanding as it is about influencing, and being influenced is a choice that those on the receiving end can make or refuse.

The power and necessity of integrity are especially clear when we consider leaders like Gandhi and Martin Luther King Jr. They had no payrolls to dispense, no available carrots and sticks like hiring, firing, and promoting. The only way they could move people to undertake the formidable, often frightening actions they believed necessary was by inspiring them to understand and choose action. The instinct for self-preservation is deep; very few people in pre-independence India or the segregation-era South would have willingly risked beatings or jail had they not believed these leaders to be decent, honest, and selflessly, authentically concerned for the greater good.

There is a clear need to help leaders think clearly about the two primary aspects of their work: dealing with people, which is addressed by the respect side of the model; and doing the tasks, which corresponds to the responsibility side of the model. Those who worked with Marcus, for example, viewed him as highly competent and intelligent, with excellent business and financial skills. They saw him as decisive, confident, results oriented, driven, and good at problem solving, presentation skills, and negotiation. He was strong in the Leadership Character qualities of accountability, courage, and self-confidence. In terms of the qualities that make up responsibility, in other words, he was a highly developed leader. But on the respect side, his direct reports felt he was good at emotional control but did not respect them for their competence or seek their input or suggestions even though they were all vice presidents with strong skill sets. He was viewed as weak in empathy, humility, and lack of blame. He was weak in respect.

Marcus needed to grow in respect, and Ed needed to grow in responsibility. Every leader needs encouragement to grow in the particular areas that can bring all core qualities of character into balance to accomplish both aspects of the job successfully. Almost always, people are stronger on one side than on the other. The scale is a graphic reminder that leading with character is a matter of keeping respect and responsibility in balance. The core qualities that generate respect and responsibility are innate in all of us, but we all have them in varying degrees. Being out of balance skews our ability to lead effectively. Every one of us must purposely and continuously develop and strengthen those core qualities to express real, balanced Leadership Character.

When we work with individual executives or a management team, we usually conduct a 360-degree assessment. In this assessment, people are rated by peers, superiors, direct reports, customers, and any others who are in a position to help give a complete and rounded view on many aspects of their behavior.

After every rating, the rater is asked to add a comment amplifying the assessment. One area in which the subjects are rated is integrity. After conducting thousands of these assessments, we found that leaders who failed to treat others with respect (lacking empathy, for example) were viewed as low in integrity. Similarly, when they behaved irresponsibly and were not accountable (for instance, failing to follow through on commitments), they were also viewed as lacking in integrity.

Here are some typical comments raters made to explain low ratings they had given in integrity. Their comments illustrate a perceived lack of respect:

- "Doesn't portray the values of the company such as respect for the individual. Shows favoritism, treats others as though they are not expected to think for themselves or are not capable. It is his way or you need to leave."

- "How could I rate him any higher when he manages his groups through domination and control and intimidation?"

And these comments about integrity reflect problems with responsibility:

- "Totally decent human being, but unresponsive managerial style is discouraging and demoralizing."

- "I didn't feel good about the way he took so long to get back to people, both to my employees and one time to a vendor who was trying to work with him. It did not represent the values of our organization."

- "I don't think he knows how much his lack of accountability and opportunistic travel schedules impact how people feel."

Being seen as weak in respect or responsibility cost those leaders their reputation for integrity in the eyes of those who evaluated them. Even though leaders may not be dishonest (literally cheating or lying), they will undermine their own Leadership Character if they blame others or fail to empathize with others (core issues of respect), or if they don't make themselves accountable or fail to follow through (core issues of responsibility). They will be perceived as having low integrity. The qualities of character are interrelated and interdependent. Real integrity that others recognize and honor is reinforced by developing the qualities inherent in respect and responsibility.

In Marcus's case, one of his direct reports felt that Marcus frequently participated at a level of detail at which he should not have been involved, sending the message that he did not trust other people's judgment and skills. Another said that Marcus conveyed an image of being concerned with employees' success only as it benefited the company, and that he felt viewed by Marcus more as a means to an end than as a person making a valuable contribution. A third direct report said that Marcus was unwilling to accommodate personal motivations different from his own, or to seek to understand others' points of view. Yet another said that Marcus needed to be less judgmental and require less minute justification for everything. This person said that people were made so anxious by Marcus that they felt unable to think things through and make decisions.

Marcus saw himself as a leader of strength and integrity. But the fact is, integrity is not just about how you see yourself. It is also about how others perceive you, and you will not be perceived as a leader with integrity unless you are both respectful and responsible.

THE IMPORTANCE OF BALANCE

When data from the 360-degree assessments are correlated with data from the individual personality inventories given to the executives we work with, the importance of balancing respect and responsibility is reinforced.

Those who score high in willingness to take risks as measured by personality assessments tend to be seen by co-workers as high in confidence and courage. High scorers are willing to say what needs to be said, question existing practices, suggest new ways of doing things, and so on. They are strong, in other words, on the responsibility side. But the data also show that those high in risk-taking are very likely to be seen by their co-workers as lacking sensitivity or emotional control, weaknesses in behavior that are associated with the character qualities of empathy and emotional mastery on the respect side of the model. These data support the notion that we are seeing two dimensions that don't naturally coexist with ease and balance.

These two dimensions of leadership (termed *task-oriented* and *people-oriented* by some theorists) were described by research begun at Ohio State University and the University of Michigan in the 1940s[1] and have been confirmed many times since—confirmed, in fact, by our own factor analysis of behavioral data on the thousands of executives we have worked with over the years.

Despite the variations in how the phenomenon was described, all of this research concludes that the types of behaviors leaders display fall consistently into two areas, which can very broadly be described as task-oriented behavior (which involves the character traits on the responsibility side of our model) and people-oriented behavior (which uses the character traits on the respect side.) In the Ohio State studies, the two behaviors were called Initiating Structure (similar to the Leadership Character Model responsibility

———

side) and Consideration (like the respect side) and were understood as separate. In this formulation, a manager could score high on both behaviors. The Michigan studies called them Production Centered (responsibility, again) and Employee Centered (respect), and saw them instead as the ends of a continuum.

Robert Kaplan and Robert Kaiser, of the leadership consultancy Kaplan DeVries, Inc., have come up with another way of naming the same two factors, calling them *forceful* and *enabling* leadership. Like us, they view these as a polarity, not a continuum. Both poles are good, both must be developed, and both must be used in a balanced way. Kaplan and Kaiser write:

> *By forceful, we mean leading off of one's intellect and energy—taking stands, being decisive, making tough calls, holding people accountable, and so on. By enabling we mean creating conditions for other people to make a contribution—granting them autonomy, being receptive to their influence, providing support, helping them feel valued.*[2]

To be a forceful leader, a person must develop the character qualities on the responsibility side of the Leadership Character scale; to be an enabling leader, a person must develop strengths on the respect side.

Whether imagined as separate or as occupying opposite ends of a continuum, two distinct sets of qualities are clearly involved in leadership, and keeping them in balance is the challenge.

HOW ED AND MARCUS GREW

Ed and Marcus's Story

Both Ed and Marcus had to make changes in their behavior to achieve balanced Leadership Character. Marcus needed to tone down his style and develop more empathy and humility. He needed to balance responsibility with respect. Ed needed to become more self-confident and assertive, stop procrastinating, and put issues on the table to get them resolved. He needed to balance his respect and concern for people's feelings with the courage to operate outside his comfort zone and hold others accountable.

At the urging of one of their board members who was a former client of ours, Marcus and Ed came to us (separately) to participate in our firm's executive development program. In this process, we first gather data on the person using individual personality inventories, a job history interview, and interviews with the boss and co-workers, as well as a 360-degree review that is completed by fifteen to twenty of the person's co-workers. We videotape an extensive life history interview; the tape is given to the person to watch, at home with a spouse or significant other, while considering a series of questions designed to help people see themselves in new ways. Then, armed with the information revealed, we work with the leader individually to identify and develop the specific qualities of leadership the person needs to strengthen.

Initially, with Marcus, we focused on his strengths, showing him in detail how each of his strengths was of incredible value to the company. We took the appropriate opportunities throughout the life history interview to value his contributions. But in the beginning, Marcus was skeptical of the benefit he would receive from the program. To suggestions of how he might shift his behavior, he would say things like, "I've tried that and it doesn't work with these people." As the coaching progressed, he began to trust our requests and experiment with some new actions, such as asking one of his direct reports for input, then finding a way to implement the person's suggestions and revisiting the person to thank him and tell him why his input was valuable and that it was really helping the company. He tried this with other direct reports and began to see the value of this very different approach.

Meanwhile, Ed told us he realized he had initially tried to appease Marcus. Then, when he tried to put the issues on the table with him, Marcus would agree to be more collaborative and less controlling, but things did not really change. Ed still believed that Marcus was the right person for the job, but he recognized that he himself was not being effective in his leadership role with Marcus. He preferred harmony to the point that he avoided conflict. He also said that he knew that he was probably viewed as a pushover by his people, even though his standards were high and he expected much of himself.

In terms of dealing with their team, this tension and difference in leadership style might show up like this: Ed would call a meeting with his staff, they would discuss issues to be resolved, and decisions would be made. But when a person did not meet a deadline, there would be no discussion or consequences; the assignment would eventually get done, but the delays often hampered others. This was a common problem until Marcus joined the company. However, when Marcus followed through with the employees on these kinds of issues, they often resented it and would complain to Ed about Marcus's micromanaging them, and Ed would let them off the hook. Ed acknowledged that his desire to be liked made him reluctant to hold others accountable, which only encouraged Marcus to overuse what should have been a strength—his dogged attention to follow-up—and resulted in his being viewed as a cop.

Although Ed agreed with Marcus's ideas, he did not like the manner—or the lack of manners—that Marcus used in implementing them. Marcus would then get upset with Ed for not backing him up, and in these discussions—actually, confrontations—he was rude to Ed. Ed's way of dealing with Marcus became to avoid meeting with him, if possible, because of his aggressiveness. He said that whenever they talked, it just made things even worse between them.

"To help break through the pattern of conflict that had developed between him and Ed," Bob recalls, "I asked Marcus to spend two weeks just listening whenever they had conversations and finding ways to show respect for the content of what Ed was saying." Now, looking back, Marcus says, "I realized I hadn't been sensitive to him. He was the founder of the company. He had been running it without me. He'd never had to give up control before, and that's a hard thing to do. It was on me to try to understand his character and persona." These turned out to be the first interactions Ed had ever had with Marcus in which he did not feel that Marcus was trying to compete with him.

"The difficult part with Ed," Bob remembers, "was getting him to try out some new ways of doing things so he could see for himself that he didn't always have to be liked." We had to get him to see that he would be respected even more when he put issues on the table as they came up and worked to get them resolved.

To begin transforming his way of interacting with his staff, we asked Ed to choose one of his direct reports to have a meeting with to discuss goals and expectations. He then set a time and date for subsequent meetings to evaluate progress toward these goals. During this time, Ed also made a point of learning more about the personalities, strengths, and weaknesses of each of his direct reports. For one of his direct reports who had difficulty meeting deadlines, he helped the person set up a structure and process for getting things done on time. He also arranged for her to work with another employee who found it easy to be organized and timely. Ed made it clear that he wanted them to work together so the other employee could serve as a peer mentor and help this person build better habits. With each of his direct reports, Ed looked at strengths and areas of difficulty, and together they developed a plan that would enable the employee to get better at those things that did not come easily.

ACHIEVING A SENSE OF MASTERY

The breakthrough for Ed was the sense of mastery he felt when he began these meetings. He realized that this was really what his people wanted from him. He realized that even when he had to be tough, the bonds he had built with his people gave him lots of "credits." As he experimented with requiring more of employees, his relationship with Marcus also improved. Marcus respected Ed more and was relieved to no longer feel he had to be the "bad guy."

And while Marcus was also making an obvious effort to be more collaborative and partnering, Ed could see how his own improvements had a positive impact on Marcus, eliciting a genuinely respectful attitude.

DOING IT DIFFERENTLY

The greatest breakthrough for Marcus came after several of our sessions. He came in and excitedly wanted to share a story about how he had handled a situation very differently than he previously would have done. A huge mistake had been made with a client, and it was going to result in a big financial loss for the company. He said that in the past he would have called a meeting and announced, "We have a big problem that is going to be very costly to us. We are all going to have to bear some of the financial burden. Nothing else can be done to correct the mistake. I don't want to hear any bellyaching about this. Each of you has to accept this and move on. Now, does everyone understand what we have to do?" And there would have been dead silence, with maybe some slight nodding of heads in agreement.

Instead of this habitual way of handling the problem, Marcus told us, he called a meeting and, when everyone was seated, said, "We have a problem. I would like to state what I see as the problem and then go around the room and have each of you state how you view it and offer any ideas you might have for what we should do." As people began discussing the problem and its possible solutions, they became animated and engaged rather than disheartened, but they stayed focused on coming up with the best solution for both parties. Marcus said that he did not talk any more himself because he did not need to. The team came up with a solution that did require the company to take a financial hit, but a smaller one than if he had conducted things in his usual dictating way and had made a decision independent of his team's ideas. He was able to see that everyone felt a sense of personal ownership because they had participated in both the problem's identification and its solution. Marcus told us that when he left the meeting, he felt so excited about what had resulted from his valuing and using the brains of his team that he actually experienced chills.

"It was a leap of faith," Marcus remembers now, "to draw on the strengths and wisdom of everybody: not to micromanage, not to feel as though I had to come up with a solution myself and announce it to the team. But it was so positive that I wanted to do more of it. Now when I am with my management team in similar situations, I really try to leverage the collective brain power."

Marcus's focus on treating others with more respect positively affected several qualities of character. He became more humble, more courageous, and less blaming. Before, for instance, his habitual approach would have caused others to feel blamed, at least indirectly. He showed courage by being willing to try what was for him an uncomfortable and risky way to solve a problem. His focus on the whole improved because now he and the company were getting the benefit of all the brainpower of the team, not just his own. Ed meanwhile became a more responsible leader, both displaying and demanding accountability, and the respectful quality of the relationships he had already built helped give him the self-confidence to do it.

USING NATURAL STRENGTHS

As Ed and Marcus came to grips with their own issues, their relationship changed for the better. Employees began to see them for the first time operating as a real partnership to drive the company forward.

"One thing I learned," Ed recalls, "was that I hadn't been playing to my strengths. As CEO, I was getting a lot of opinions from the other executives about what they would do in my position. Much of their input was negative—that I had become somewhat indecisive. But one of the big surprises was discovering that I was doing a lot of things right. In the 360-degree feedback process, I heard that even if people didn't always agree with me, they still had confidence in me and trusted my ability to make decisions. That was great to hear. I began having more confidence in my decision-making abilities and started taking action on things with less delay."

———

Ed began using his talents in more productive ways. He was proactive in building key customer and supplier relationships, wrote a best-selling book in his field, and toured the country on behalf of the company. Internally, he became a more decisive chief executive, resolving issues without delay. Marcus was still as passionate as ever about requiring accountability but was now getting more of what he wanted from both Ed and those who worked for and with him. He found that by valuing others' ideas and really operating as part of a team he accomplished much more than he could ever accomplish on his own. A short time later, Ed's company undertook an advantageous merger; Ed and Marcus agreed that the merger could have never happened had they not transformed their relationship.

• • •

The sort of conflict that existed between Marcus and Ed is extremely common in working relationships. How they transformed this dynamic illustrates our understanding of how people and organizations change: that when one person improves in attitude and behavior, it positively affects everyone else around; and that becoming stronger in any of the qualities of Leadership Character will help strengthen and balance them all. Let's take a look at one organization where character and integrity are pervasive.

HIGH INTEGRITY=HIGH MORALE=HIGH PERFORMANCE

BellSouth at Fleming Island

BellSouth's Fleming Island operation services the corporation's wholesale customers, small local exchanges and huge telecom entities alike, that buy access to BellSouth's network. Walking into the facility, south of Jacksonville, Florida, you know immediately that you're not in an ordinary corporate environment. Carolyn Howle, the security guard at the front desk, welcomes you more like the concierge at a first-class hotel. It's rare to find a place where so many people seem to be doing such good work and enjoying it and each other so thoroughly. Results are high at Fleming Island. Orders for new service get filled quickly and accurately. Customers calling for repair have short wait times, and every customer is treated with courtesy and professionalism. Morale is high. People seem energized, happy, and engaged.

When we made a visit there, we were given astonishingly free access. We talked with Mark Butterworth, who heads the operation, and with the four managers who report to him, Ron Brooks, David Pugh, Abdul Kosoko, and Karr McLeod. We also talked privately with a number of employees on the front line.

Every manager we talked with seemed committed to building trust, showing respect, and also focusing strongly on performance and responsibility. They set a palpable tone of concern for their customers. Most impressive, though, was how much Leadership Character they bring out in everyone within the organization. When we asked line workers for their feelings about management, the answers were consistent. "They respect you as an individual." "They treat you like an adult, not like a wayward child." "They have confidence in you." "They take a personal interest—they ask where you want to be five years from now." This pervasive sense of both respect and responsibility yields powerful results. Employees want to go beyond their job descriptions. All have a sense of ownership for success of the organization.

BUILDING ON A FOUNDATION OF TRUST AND OPENNESS

Ron believes that this high level of mutual trust is created by open, honest communication. "There are no hidden agendas. We believe that the truth will set you free. There are no secrets. If someone asks me a question, I say either 'I don't know,' 'I know but I can't tell you,' or 'Here's the answer.'" Fleming Island managers like Ron don't just have an open door policy; most are out on the floor with employees throughout the day. Telephones go with them, so they can take calls from anywhere.

The environment is "information rich." No one here is likely to first hear something about BellSouth from the newspaper, or as a rumor from a fellow employee. The year begins with a strategy alignment session called "Connecting the Dots," where managers share plans, talk about where the company is going, and determine how Fleming Island and each department fit in. When corporate leaders come to visit, Mark always asks them to give a "State of the State" address. Articles about BellSouth are posted on bulletin boards; while at her post, Carolyn, the security guard, scans the *Wall Street Journal* and business magazines for relevant clippings.

ELICITING RESPECT THROUGH COMMITMENT

This atmosphere of open communication creates trust and demonstrates to associates that they are respected members of the team. It also helps associates make better decisions day-to-day, because they understand their roles in the overall scheme of things. That allows them to take their jobs seriously.

The culture of respect is also demonstrated by the empathy managers seem to have for the situations, personal and professional, of their employees; by the humility they express when listening to ideas and acting on them; and by the appreciation they show when people do things right. Performance problems are dealt with quickly but courteously. As an associate said, "If you're not doing what's expected, it's dealt with. But if you don't have the knowledge, you'll get coaching and help. Managers here realize people make mistakes, and they'll say, 'Let's tear this apart, see what happened, and figure out how we can fix it.'" Respect for people's personal lives shows up in the way overtime is dealt with. When extra work is needed, if possible, volunteers are requested; typically more than enough volunteer. As Ron said, "People here know we care, so they are willing to help. We recently had a big software problem. We had to apply a fix to numerous accounts, with little time. I told my group—59 people—that we really needed help. Fifty volunteered to stay late; the other nine came up to say there were things they just couldn't get out of. We fixed the problem quickly, and not one customer lost service."

Managers are all called by their first names. Skip-level meetings, in which managers "skip over" their direct reports to meet with employees a level below, are frequent. Cross-training and temporary job swapping help people focus on the whole operation and develop empathy for the perspectives of people in other parts of the organization. "Walk in My Moccasins" days are one mechanism they use to accomplish that broader perspective. Another is moving frontline supervisors to other departments for an entire year so they can fully experience the challenges of their counterparts.

ENCOURAGING AND REWARDING GOOD IDEAS

Managers truly listen to the ideas of employees, and there are structured methods in place to encourage this. A standing focus group is activated whenever there is a need for ideas or discussion. The focus group, randomly selected and all nonmanagement, is changed every three months. There is also a formal suggestion system. Karr described it: "We have a suggestion book, and we put all our ideas in it, along with the disposition. We follow up religiously. If a suggestion isn't used, we explain why."

This receptivity to the ideas of employees has paid off in many ways. For example, soon after he was hired, Sheldon Archambault, a technician who works in provisioning (putting in place circuits and other facilities needed for new service), wanted to do "more than his job," and management supported that. He has since developed a software program to aid provisioning, for which a patent is pending.

Recognition and awards are frequent. As Mark says, "We work at catching people doing something right." There's an Employee of the Month who gets not only an award but a privileged parking space near the front door. It appears that just about anything that can be measured warrants an award program here. If do your best and then some, they pat you on the back; they even rewarded someone who worked very hard but didn't get numbers results with an "unsung hero" award. A Fleming Island logo was designed, and recognition photos are taken in front of it. The reinforcement makes associates feel respected and honored, but it also tends to increase the kind of behavior desired. Fleming Island has had numerous winners in BellSouth's company-wide "The Customer Rules!" employee award program, not only because the quality of work is deserving but also because managers make certain they take the time to write up the nominations. Praise is given publicly, but problems are dealt with in private.

Another index of what's right at Fleming Island is the constructive, mutually accountable relationship between management and the Communication Workers of America, the union that represents the bulk of BellSouth employees. Creating a cooperative management-union relationship is no easy task, but Larry Healan, the union vice president, contributes at times to the Fleming Island monthly newsletter, and his columns in the CWA newsletter, *Hotwire*, reflect the union-management collaboration.

ATTAINING PRODUCTIVITY THROUGH COMMITMENT

While the respect for and among Fleming Island associates is plain to see, there is no sloughing off here. People are focused and working. In the call centers, displays that track results loom large. Looking deeper, one sees a lot of cross-training and cross-placement between provisioning and maintenance. If maintenance has a problem with the way a circuit is benchmarked, there's good communication back to provisioning. Members of both groups also know what goes on in the Local Carrier Service Center, so they can talk to call center operators about the way orders are written up. Associates in the call center have also helped design their own performance management forms.

An in-house call management system was developed by Rodney Edwards and Kevin Gartner, two people in system administration. The system, Clairvoyant, can pull reports to see what kinds of calls are most frequent and what needs fixing. Now it's also being used throughout the department. Also manifesting the commitment to responsibility are the service order accuracy (SOA) teams. Reps with the best results move to an SOA team for three months, to review orders and give feedback and coaching to other reps, and to do what they can to improve the overall process. They point out the most common errors each associate is making and also pinpoint those that everyone is most likely to make; those problems become targets for process improvement. When they return to their regular jobs, they serve as mentors for others. An impressive expression of the individual responsibility people want to take at Fleming Island is the fact that call center associates actually *ask* for observations and reviews to be done, to improve their performance for the good of the organization and its customers.

This is a place where people want to work, and where they work well. Respect and responsibility are both strong, in balance, and grounded in integrity. The tone is set by Mark, the top leader, who actively models Leadership Character: he has high integrity, a strong sense of respect for every person, and an insistence on performance and results. He makes it clear that this is an organization with a sense of urgency and a powerful commitment to customers. That "get it done and get it done right" attitude pervades the operation. Fleming Island is a model of Leadership Character.

Key Concepts

- Integrity, the foundation of Leadership Character, is a core leadership quality that everyone can develop.

- To be a person of integrity, it's not enough to think it of yourself; everyone you deal with—peers, superiors, direct reports, customers, family members, and friends—rates you on it, too.

- The Leadership Character Model can guide your process of growth, help you understand and improve relationships, and create vibrant organizational culture.

- When you develop your own Leadership Character, the integrity of your organization grows, too.

PART TWO

RESPECT—
THE WILL TO
UNDERSTAND

3

Empathy

A cartoon accompanying a 2002 article in *Fortune* about the flaws in corporate culture that led to spectacular ethical and financial failures at companies like Enron and Global Crossing makes an eloquent point about the importance of respect, though it doesn't even have a caption.[1] A scowling, fist-pounding boss sits facing a window. Outside, a wild thunderstorm rages, but he can't see it because two employees are blocking his view with a picture of blue sky and a cheerful sun. They wear the meek, ingratiating smiles you see on frightened dogs, expressions that beg, "Please don't beat me." What's wrong with this picture? Fear, pretense, misuse of power—and likely disaster—jump off the page. Respect is nowhere to be seen.

Without respect, leaders easily come on too strong. They don't step back and reflect. They get too focused on their own agendas, or on the task at hand. They don't pay attention to other people's reactions or to other people's humanity. In fact, when we first began to develop the Leadership Character Model, we used the term *equity* where we now use *respect* to describe the qualities of empathy, emotional mastery, lack of blame, and humility. Why? Because anyone who wants to lead must see others as equal in their essential humanity, despite whatever real differences exist in power and position. It's more than being nice. It's the only way to ensure that people everywhere in the hierarchy, even at the bottom, feel confident enough to speak honestly and openly and are able to make their best contributions.

The power of respect became clear to us back in the early '80s, when we had a private practice in psychology, before we began to concentrate on leadership development. We also did social security disability testing, evaluating people who typically had either severe mental illnesses, such as schizophrenia, or other conditions, such as brain damage, retardation, or physical injury. The clients were usually on the bottom rungs socially: poor, sometimes homeless, accustomed to the near-invisibility of the "take a number and wait your turn" atmosphere of social service bureaucracies. Naturally enough, in coming to our office, many seemed anxious and suspicious.

At this time, we were part of a Sunday school class that looked at local mission needs in our community. One week, a visitor from a shelter program for homeless men spoke to the class about the power of hospitality, for which, of course, respect is a prerequisite. Hospitality, he explained, transformed his program's clients. Just being made to feel accepted and welcome allowed these troubled, beaten-down men to relax. Their eyes became unglazed. They were more able to articulate their needs, and often to move toward taking responsibility for themselves.

We decided to apply the idea of hospitality in our work with Social Security clients. We kept magazines that we thought they would enjoy in the waiting room. We had a phone there that they could use. When they arrived, we offered them coffee and served it to them. Many were unable to get child care, so we had toys to keep the children occupied. We were amazed by how cooperative and warm these clients became once they were treated with simple decency, and how open they were to telling their stories. They tried hard and even seemed to enjoy what was objectively an arduous testing experience because they felt that we wanted them to be there, and that they had a right to be present. Once we heard their stories, it was impossible for us not to empathize with them and

---

even feel a sense of closeness, despite the vast differences in our comparative situations. There's a lesson in this for any manager about how to create relationships. Recognition of the humanity of the other person is critical for establishing influence and leadership. And empathy—being able to feel with the other person—is the first step in creating that attitude of respect.

COMMUNICATION

Treating others with disrespect will quickly get you viewed as lacking in integrity. Our client Inga learned that hard lesson.

A longtime member of the sales team at a printing company, Inga was a rainmaker. She was terrific at sales and excellent at building outside relationships that brought in volumes of business. Then she was promoted to executive vice president. In her new position, she worked effectively with the other senior leaders and with board members. Her CEO hoped to groom her to succeed him, but he had one big concern: Inga's relationships with her direct reports, the salespeople with whom she had formerly worked as an equal, had become strained. Because she felt unsure in her new role after ascending to a position of power over people who had been her peers, Inga became a bit of a bully.

"I had been together with the other salespeople as peers for ten years," she says now, "and I didn't realize how significantly that would have to change. I had never had any formal management training. I was winging it, but trying to manage these relationships in the same way I had operated as a peer just didn't work."

The way she managed her people was mostly by making them feel as though they could never measure up. Bob recalls, "One afternoon when Inga came in, she constantly focused on what was wrong. It was very difficult for anybody to please her."

"I didn't understand that the communication you have with your peers can be offhand and indirect and unintentional," Inga says, "but once you can hire and fire them, there's a lot more seriousness to it. From a leadership standpoint, communication is everything. It's got to be crystal clear and consistent. Your words have a lot more weight. You can't make a comment about the way a person dresses, for instance, without that being an indictment.

"I'm a very direct person. I used to assume that other people accepted that as honest, open communication, but a lot of it they just took to be insensitive, and even unkind."

Bob recalls that Inga felt her people weren't being accountable, but he could tell she wasn't considering where they were coming from or the effect her actions and language might be having on them. Even though she considered herself an honest and straightforward person, her subordinates couldn't help but think, "If she had real integrity, she wouldn't treat us this way." Our challenge was to get Inga to see that she would get increased accountability by changing the way she talked with and about her direct reports, as well as how she felt about them; she needed to treat them with empathy. Later in this chapter, we'll see how Inga was able to change.

THE ESSENCE OF EMPATHY

Empathy is the ability to recognize emotions in other people. It is feeling *with* someone. It implies and requires a sense of equality. It's different from sympathy, which is feeling *for* someone, often specifically feeling sorry for someone, which is more likely to be the result of an inequality of circumstances. Sympathy is detached; empathy is connected.

To be empathetic, you don't need to believe that the other person's feelings are logical or justified, and you don't need to *act* in any way that is motivated by another's feelings. Empathy does not make you compromise your own feelings, or your better judgment either. But it does require you to make an imaginative leap that allows you to *know* what the other person is feeling, and why.

You often hear people say, when describing why they have chosen a particular person as a life partner, that above and beyond many other reasons, "My partner understands me in a way nobody else seems to be able to." That's a measure of the deep hunger people have to be understood, and it shows why empathy is so powerful in relationships.

People who are empathetic are attuned to the subtle social signals that indicate what others need or want. They are powerful listeners. They are also sensitive to how they themselves are perceived. They may be forceful, and they may have big ideas about themselves and their role in the organization or even the world, but they are not arrogant or judgmental toward others because their skills at empathy always let them see themselves in the other person's situation.

"No one is a leader who can't put himself or herself in the other person's shoes,"[2] wrote Gus Pagonis, a former lieutenant general in the U.S. Army who headed logistics during the first Gulf War and later became head of logistics at Sears. Pagonis talks about how vital empathy was to him as a manager in the complex, pressured context of war. He asked himself questions like, What do the other people on our team need? Why do they think they need it, and how can we give it to them? Questions like this keep a leader thinking from the point of view of the other.

During his army service, Pagonis noticed a bad habit in himself: while talking with subordinates, he would sift quickly through the mail or paperwork on his desk. Eventually, he realized that poor listening skills often prevented him from truly understanding others and made people feel he didn't respect them. So he started making a point of maintaining eye contact with the person he was talking with.

Pagonis also used empathy to deal with his hosts, the Saudis. Having half a million American troops in a strict Muslim country wasn't easy, and it required sensitive diplomacy. The Saudis were bothered by women soldiers unloading crates, bareheaded and with their sleeves rolled up. Because he was able to put himself in the Saudis' place, to see the problem from their perspective, Pagonis found a solution that worked for both sides: when outside and in view, all soldiers would wear long-sleeved shirts, and women would wear caps. This minor trade-off yielded major diplomatic gains.

It would be hard to find a better model of empathy than the children's television personality Fred Rogers. Less than a year before he died in 2003, we were lucky to hear him speak to an audience made up primarily of high-level executives at a national conference of United Way donors. Along with his talk, Rogers showed video clips of some of his favorite interactions with kids over the years. By the time he finished, there was not a dry eye in the audience. How was this mild, soft-spoken man able to so powerfully affect an auditorium full of movers and shakers? In just the same way he had touched and won the confidence of generations of children. For children, his mass media broadcast seemed more like a private chat. They genuinely felt he was part of their world, and that he understood how they felt. Most of us lose that sensitivity in adulthood and consequently lack the ability to make another person feel really understood.

Bob spoke with Rogers after his speech. "He never looked away, never looked over my shoulder for somebody more important. He didn't act as though he was more important than I. I felt that he was interested in what I said, and that we had known each other for a long time." When he died, we were touched to read in an obituary that he always carried in his wallet this quote from a Benedictine nun: "There's no one you can't love, once you've heard their story." It is in letting ourselves listen to others that we acknowledge them as people, put them on an equal footing with ourselves, let them move us. And that makes it possible for us to move them.

Empathy is essential for forming relationships of influence with anyone. It's critical, for example, in childrearing, where the way that parents listen and respond makes a huge difference in the quality of their relationships with their kids. Lyn has always been especially fascinated to observe parents with young kids at the grocery store. She says she has seen this a million times, and you probably have, too: The child points and says, "Cookie!" or tries to pull a box off the shelf and into the cart. Some parents will just ignore the kid or answer harshly, "No, we're not getting those." Lyn

---

says it's not often that you see a more engaged, empathetic mother or father who says something like, "Yes, sweetie, that's a cookie, but we can't get any today. They look good, though, don't they?" Either way, the kid doesn't get the cookie. But one child's desire is heard and acknowledged, while the other one's wish is just squelched. These communication patterns are established early, but they affect parent-child relationships for a lifetime.

We're certainly not perfect parents, but we have tried to be conscious of these dynamics. There was a time when Lyn had just made a pledge to herself to try to be a better listener: to paraphrase and reflect when listening rather than quickly jumping to offer advice. One day our son Rob, who was about eleven, came in from school obviously upset. He slammed his book bag on the kitchen table. The exchange went something like this:

> **Lyn:** Rob, what's wrong?
> **Rob:** Somebody stole the bats, and now we have to do exercises in P.E. instead of softball.
> **Lyn:** Oh, that's too bad. And that's your favorite part of the day.
> **Rob:** Yeah, and the coach won't even let the rest of us pay to buy new ones. He says whoever took them has to bring them back.

Lyn was sorely tempted at this point to launch into a mini-lecture about why the coach would have said this, but she remembered her pledge.

> **Lyn:** Oh, Rob, I'm so sorry. If he changes his mind, I'll contribute toward the new bats.
> **Rob:** That's OK. I can understand. If we just paid for new ones, it wouldn't teach them a lesson.

And then he took his books upstairs and went out to play.

Lyn is still amazed by that reaction. If she had reacted with a lecture instead of with empathy, would Rob have argued and stayed angry, and would she ever have heard that mature response? Lyn and Rob both grew in that interchange. Empathy is a powerful teacher.

EMOTIONAL INTELLIGENCE
AND EMPATHY

The old-style leaders who moved to top levels in organizations usually had an ability to manage upward and could also relate well outward, to customers. They often, however, lacked real empathy; they didn't spend a lot of time reflecting on their impact on others. Research by the Center for Creative Leadership, confirmed by our own investigation, shows that arrogance and the inability to manage relationships with others are the top causes of the derailment of executives' careers.[3] That old, insensitive style simply doesn't cut it anymore. (We'll talk more about this later, in the chapter on humility.) When comparing the leaders we have coached who were rated highest by their co-workers with those rated lowest, there is almost no difference in technical skill. The greatest differences are seen in the abilities to facilitate teamwork, to motivate others, and to be an inspirational role model.

These are important elements of what Daniel Goleman has aptly termed *emotional intelligence,* noncognitive abilities that allow us to manage ourselves and to manage relationships effectively. Goleman reports on research by the late David McClelland, a noted Harvard University psychologist, in which McClelland showed that the divisions of a large food and beverage company led by managers who scored high on emotional intelligence "outperformed yearly revenue targets by 15 percent to 20 percent." Conversely, those managers who scored low on emotional intelligence "rarely rated as outstanding in their annual performance reviews, and their divisions under-performed by an average of almost 20 percent."[4] Goleman has spent years studying the contribution of emotional intelligence to performance and has found it more important than technical or cognitive skills at all levels of leadership. He has found it even more crucial at higher levels of leadership. "When I compared star performers with average ones in senior leadership positions, nearly 90 percent of the difference in their profiles was attributable to emotional intelligence factors rather than cognitive abilities."[5]

———

People with emotional intelligence are both self-aware and sensitive to the feelings of others. Their understanding of human feelings and their ability to form lasting relationships with their employees and customers are much more developed than they are in those who lack this quality. These empathetic individuals are able to read people's reactions and motivate them by recognizing what's important to them. They can tell whether employees are challenged and engaged, and they understand why that is desirable. According to research by Gallup, one of the twelve questions people use in deciding whether stay with or leave an organization is, "Does my supervisor or someone at work seem to care about me as a person?"[6] That's another way of asking to be treated with empathy.

Empathy is essential for using what Goleman calls "resonance." The term is borrowed from music, where it connotes the reinforcement or prolonging of a sound; think of echoing. Scientists are now recognizing that humans "catch" emotions from each other. We pick up mood and tone especially from leaders, because leaders are the people we watch and emulate. Upbeat leaders produce energy and confidence in others; that's resonance. Cross, negative leaders produce followers who are also irritable and anxious; Goleman calls this "dissonance." A leader's emotions are inevitably going to influence the feelings of the people who report to her; whether to let this happen unconsciously or to use the dynamic in a deliberate, creative, and resonant way is her choice. Leaders with emotional intelligence are able both to monitor and manage their own emotions and to recognize, through the social astuteness that comes from empathy, the emotions they are creating in others. Goleman writes:

> *Quite simply, in any human group the leader has maximal power to sway everyone's emotions. If people's emotions are pushed toward the range of enthusiasm, performance can soar; if people are driven toward rancor and anxiety, they will be thrown off stride.*[7]

HOW EMPATHETIC LEADERSHIP
STRENGTHENS ORGANIZATIONS

The advantage of having a high degree of empathy is that you are able to connect with others at a deep level. That's important in business or in any organization because it works like a magnet. If people are drawn to you and comfortable with you, if they feel you have an openness, they also know that you will understand them and they will be open toward you. They want to confide in you, tell you what's going on—even give you bad news. So you get much more feedback, which you must have to be an effective leader. You will not find yourself in the risky position of that boss in the cartoon described at the beginning of this chapter, who has frightened his employees into telling him only what he wants to hear.

A lack of empathy makes it difficult to build teams. If a leader's language and actions don't reflect an understanding of others' issues, the atmosphere of the team won't facilitate strong, open communication. Often, when a leader of a team is low in empathy, we see conflict manifested within the group in the form of aggressive behavior, and constructive methods for resolution are also usually lacking. Alternatively, we might see conflict being avoided because working out difficult issues would require more openness and discussion of feelings than the leader has modeled and created space for. There is no room in such a group for constructive conflict.

Empathy also increases a person's ability in negotiation because the goal of good negotiation is to create win-win situations, where both parties can come away with something of benefit. A truly successful negotiation results in a solution that is synergistic and superior to the singular position of either side. If you are in a negotiation, the first and most important challenge for you is to convey to the other parties that you can see the matter from their perspective. Beyond that, you must be able to discuss the issues in a way that allows the other side to say to themselves that you really do understand their position. When they can tell themselves that, your credibility is established, as is your ability to have influence.

In situations of conflict, or stymied negotiation, you often hear unproductive conversations that seem to lead nowhere. Sometimes the parties don't even seem to be engaged in quite the same dialogue. That's why when negotiation skills are taught in training programs, a simulation is often done in which each person must first paraphrase and reflect back what the other has said before being allowed to make any new point or to try to further the conversation. This is a way to get practice in empathizing, and in demonstrating that you have heard and understood the other person. Now this simulated exchange may be a little forced and artificial when compared to real conversations, but the fact that exercises like this are done repeatedly in business training all over the world shows how very important empathy is considered to be.

EMPATHY CAN BE LEARNED

Researchers believe that to a great degree a person's IQ, or intelligence quotient, is more or less fixed, but one's emotional intelligence and its constituent elements, including empathy, can be cultivated and enhanced. Just as aptitudes can vary for, say, acquiring technical knowledge (which is why some of us are quick studies when it comes to learning new software and others feel challenged or even overwhelmed by that kind of task), we all have different strengths and weaknesses in relating to other people. But with determination and practice we can improve those skills.

Daniel Goleman describes a Wall Street executive who was shocked to learn that people at work were afraid of his insensitivity and, to protect themselves, shielded him from bad news.[8] It upset him even more when his own family members told him they felt and acted the same way. Working with a coach, he came to see that he needed to improve his ability to read other people's reactions and to recognize their perspectives. His desire to change was so strong that he spent a week in a country where he did not speak the language, just so he could observe himself in confusing and unfamiliar situations. He also began observing and modeling people who listened well and had the coach shadow him to give him feedback on his response to people who had different ideas or perspectives. He had himself videotaped in meetings and had those who worked for him give feedback on his ability to acknowledge and understand the feelings of others. As a result of this concerted effort, his skills of empathy developed. His relationships improved, and so did his performance.

You may not be in a position to spend a week in a foreign country, but there are things you can decide to do that will help you develop your skills of empathy.

- **Practice perspective taking.** Part of empathy is the ability to take the perspective of the other, as Gus Pagonis had to do with the Saudis during the Gulf War. To develop your perspective-taking skills, constantly try to figure out how another person would describe a situation. For example, if you're in a sales organization, think about how someone would describe a problem you're having with a product from a marketing point of view. Or you can play "Pick a Character, Tell the Story." To do that, read a novel or business case study, or watch a movie. Then pick one of the characters and tell the story from that character's point of view. Doing that repeatedly, especially with characters you don't particularly like, will hone your perspective-taking skills.

- **Develop your inquiry skills.** Peter Senge, founder of the Society for Organizational Learning, contends in his classic book, *The Fifth Discipline*, that skillful discussion requires balancing inquiry and advocacy.[9] Inquiry skills can help you develop your ability to take the perspective of the other, which cultivates empathy. Inquiry means exploring another person's ideas in a way that allows you to really understand his or her opinion, rather than simply quickly giving back your own ideas, which is what we most often do. Putting forward your own ideas is called advocacy. Both inquiry and advocacy are important, but too much advocacy makes for a ping-pong discussion where no consensus is reached, and too much inquiry creates a situation where no one ever steps forward to say, "I think we should do this." Groups reach decisions faster when inquiry and advocacy are balanced.

Real inquiry demands and shows tremendous respect for others and their ideas but unfortunately tends to be lacking. The next time you are in a meeting, put your own opinion on hold long enough to explore what others are offering. Let yourself be curious and ask questions. We have found that balancing inquiry and advocacy is extremely helpful in working with executive teams. No other single concept has done more to help these collections of strong-willed people shift their process from unproductive competition to collaborative discussion that can yield productive decisions.

- **Read to develop empathy.** We think in stories. The people who write them well have enormous powers of empathy; how else could they put themselves inside their characters and convey emotions so well? Reading stories about people who have believable feelings, whether they are real or fictional characters, can help us to develop empathy, too. In a sense, reading allows us to occupy the same emotional space as the writer. Seek out memoirs or character-driven nonfiction titles: *Angela's Ashes* and *Schindler's List* are two books whose vivid characters touched us powerfully. Read novels with strong character development, like *A Map of the World*. If you have young children, get Jim Trelease's *Read Aloud Handbook*, and read the recommended books to your kids.[10] Trelease says that we are born knowing how to cry for ourselves; through reading we learn to cry for others.

LEARNING TO LISTEN

Angelo's Story

Angelo's appointment as the manager of a unit in a Fortune 500 telecommunications company came with some stress; his previous position, which had been done away with, had carried more responsibility. "In addition to my concerns about how that might be perceived by others in the company," he recalls, "I was just too self-centered, too worried about what people thought of me, and too involved in trying to make myself look good."

Angelo became concerned that his new team was not gelling, and that his leadership wasn't being accepted by his direct reports. He felt he had to come on strong to create a sense of urgency. In a meeting with his direct reports, for example, one of them had not completed an assignment, and Angelo let himself become visibly upset with this person. Other members of the team were obviously made uncomfortable and he hoped this would help motivate them to not make the same mistake.

"I wasn't an inspirational leader," he says now. "I used sarcasm and lampooning. I didn't consciously try to make people feel bad. Being quick-witted and a smart aleck was learned behavior that had worked for me in the past." When Angelo entered our executive development program and received the feedback from his 360-degree assessment, he was surprised that so many people mentioned his caustic humor as being inappropriate. "This was a point in my life where it wasn't working anymore. People thought I lacked sensitivity."

When he began to work on developing more empathy, viewing himself from other people's perspective, the situation began to improve. He worked hard to eliminate the caustic humor, and when he did use humor, it was no longer biting.

"My coaching sessions made me realize that I have this high impulsivity factor. I'm very impatient. Bob told me, 'You need to reflect before you speak.' The other key word he gave me was *reframe.* So when I heard something I might once have automatically taken in a certain way, and right away started developing my answer—or my defense—I began to ask, 'What did you mean?' Maybe I'd find out I wasn't being attacked, and that there was a legitimate issue. Reflect and reframe. That made me very self-aware. Even if I couldn't stop myself from reacting, I would hear myself and think about what I said and realize, 'That could be

———

taken wrong.' There started to be instances when I was able to correct something I'd just said, right on the spot. I really made a conscious effort.

"I had *reflect and reframe* written on my portfolio. In one meeting I took a pen and made stroke tallies every time I had the impulse to say something but didn't. My page started filling up with stroke tallies. After that meeting, my boss told me I'd really hit a home run; that it was the best meeting he'd ever seen me do; that I'd come off professionally and used humor when appropriate but didn't overdo it.

"The people that I admired most always demonstrated the qualities in the Leadership Character Model we used in our sessions. Those are the qualities I value. My self-opinion was, 'I'm as solid as a rock; I should be somebody people look up to.' So when I got feedback that I was lacking these attributes, I saw behaviors I needed to change."

Angelo held one-on-one meetings with each of his direct reports. He talked about the relationships and ways he had treated them that, upon reflection, he saw were not in the best interest of the person or the team. Modeling that kind of vulnerability and openness caused his team members to begin to view him differently. Tension and distance that had existed began to clear up. Angelo says that working on empathy and changing how he related to his people also helped him improve his emotional mastery and humility, and to move beyond blaming. "I used to do unto others as I would want to have done unto me. But now I believe I should do unto them as they want to be done to."

• • •

LEARNING TO HEAR YOURSELF SPEAK

Inga's Story

Remember Inga, who when promoted to lead the printing company sales department treated her former peers as if they just couldn't measure up? The comments people made in her 360-degree review made a big impression. "I cried," she remembers. "It was heartbreaking to me, that everybody felt that way." Viewing her videotaped interview also brought the message home. She would say later that this was a life-changing event. She could see herself being animated, excited, and positive when talking about her peers, her boss, or people in the other organizations she was working with to bring in business. She recognized herself as inspiring and motivating in those situations. But when she began talking about her own people, she saw that she moved to the edge of her seat, changed her tone, and in every case talked about what was wrong with each one. "When I saw myself the way the people around me saw me," she recalls, "it was an eye-opener."

Bob used empathy to help Inga develop it in herself, making clear that he understood her motives and goals. He told her he knew feeling heartbroken was painful, but that it was actually helpful to this process. It showed her capacity for the empathy she needed in order to make her people feel valued. He made it clear to Inga that he really believed that her motives were coming from a desire to do a good job, but that she had a blind spot, and how fortunate she was to now see through a new lens.

"I never had the friendship orientation with people I reported to," Inga says now, in explaining why she related so well to those above her while relating so poorly to those below. "So there was always a decorum. The issue with the salespeople is that we had been together as peers for ten years, and I didn't realize how significantly that would have to change. I had to reposition myself. It was tough. You have to build on the history of friendship, but you have to change it. That was the revelation for me.

"So the social time became much more focused and equitable. If I took one out to dinner, I had to take each one out to dinner. We had tickets to an outdoor summer concert series. Before, if I went with salesperson A and her client, it seemed fine. But I had to not show favoritism."

———

As her coaching sessions progressed, Inga would come in excited about having been able to demonstrate how she had been empathetic with a direct report: by listening to the person, taking the information and then reflecting back what the person said to be sure he knew she understood the issues and concerns, and proceeding in a mutual problem-solving way so that the person felt support—that they were partners in a relationship. "I started understanding team dynamics," she says. "I did a better job of reinforcing and validating my people and helping them play to their strengths. I begin to first think 'in their shoes' and second ask myself how to communicate based on who they are, where they are, and what filters they might be using to hear the information."

Inga's image of herself became one of a developer of people. She began to take pleasure in helping those who reported to her and worked around her to grow in their thinking, behavior, and actions. When the CEO retired, she was made his successor. Since then she has moved on to found her own management consulting business, as well as a women's mentoring organization. "I've been effective at it because part of what I'm doing is working with leadership teams and applying a lot of the things I learned in my own Leadership Character development sessions. I'm a much better leader now because I'm aware of my own style. Perception is reality. I expected that people would understand the intention of my heart, but all they can do is draw conclusions from what they see me do and say. Before, I wasn't *intentionally* unempathetic; I was *unconsciously* unempathetic. I didn't have to change my heart. I just had to change my style."

◆ ◆ ◆

Empathy allows you to connect with people, to understand them, and ultimately to influence them. It makes conflict a creative process and is the key to successful negotiation. As both Angelo and Inga found out, it's a skill you can consciously develop and then use to become a more powerful leader.

Key Concepts

- Empathy is the ability to recognize what another person is feeling, and why.

- Showing empathy involves learning to take perspective, to ask questions for the sake of inquiry, and to listen for understanding, as well as to develop your own self-awareness.

- Genuine empathy enables you to gather better information, build stronger teams, and influence others successfully.

4

Emotional Mastery

S teve, the vice president for development at a software company, had a typically autocratic style of leadership. He may not have realized it, but he was a subscriber to Theory X, believing that people are inherently lazy and it is up to a manager to stay on them all the time to get any work out of them. At the same time, he found it difficult to give useful feedback. He tended to fume and then blow up. "I did not have the emotional fortitude to give constructive criticism," he says now. He often didn't get the results he wanted, either.

Steve's direct reports described his behavior as bullying. Once, for instance, someone made a mistake that Steve became aware of. This employee was talking with other employees in the hallway when Steve walked up and confronted him, angrily and loudly. At meetings with his team of seven directors, Steve would use language that was intimidating, demeaning, and sarcastic.

Steve's outbursts had a negative effect. People often wouldn't tell him when there was a problem with a customer or a defect in a product until the situation reached crisis proportions. No one wanted to be the bearer of bad news for fear of his reaction.

Steve's rationale was that if he didn't push his people, they would never accomplish what was necessary for the business to compete successfully. He was a production-driven, results-focused person, and though he genuinely believed that he was doing the right thing, "I could not correct behavior or negotiate effectively," he says now. "I would either get emotional and overreact or become passive. I would say to myself, 'If they don't appreciate my contribution and don't want to take my advice, then let them suffer the consequences,' which, I was confident, would be negative." When Steve took steps to get help, it became clear right away that he had a classic problem with emotional mastery.

Jamal, vice president of a business unit in a major automotive manufacturing company, also had a problem with emotional mastery, but one that manifested quite differently. For Jamal, it came out not as bullying but as anxiety and internalized anger, and its source was the fact that despite his professional successes, he viewed himself as a victim.

When Jamal first came to us, he was quite bothered. His unit, which he had helped found and which had become a valuable profit center, had been merged with a smaller one. He had been passed over in the choice of president for the combined unit. He felt that he had put in a tremendous amount of effort and was well qualified, and the person who got the job was quite a bit younger, had served less time with the company, and had no experience within Jamal's unit. Rather than looking for objective reasons that might explain why he had not been chosen, Jamal became anxious and angry and felt the company had taken advantage of him. He projected blame.

Jamal even had a victim attitude regarding his unit, as though it were a stepchild of the parent company. He unwittingly conveyed this feeling to his staff, and they in turn adopted a similar attitude. It would come out in grumbling expressions like, "We have to fight for everything we get around here."

In fact, when the officers of the corporation were considering whom to promote, they concluded that Jamal was too territorial and not collaborative enough across the company. Though the financial performance of his unit was good, Jamal was viewed as not requiring enough of his people, and as erring on the side of a narrow view of loyalty. His superiors saw him as "circling the wagons" to protect his people from outside harm, more than holding them accountable to the organization as a whole.

MANAGING YOUR EMOTIONS

Though it showed up very differently in each of them, both Steve and Jamal had problems controlling their anger. Steve most often expressed it openly in tirades and Jamal let it seep out as resentment. No matter how it's expressed, anger gets in the way of respectful relationships. As Jack Welch, former CEO of GE, has said, "Trust and respect take years to build, and no time at all to destroy."[1] Perhaps the most common way respect is destroyed is by displays of anger. Controlling your emotions is critical to a culture of respect.

There are challenges in every person's life, and every organization is subject to times of urgency and stress, whether arising from internal mistakes or external circumstances that can't be controlled. Feeling pressured at those times is a natural response; every healthy, resilient organization has internal debates and differences of opinion. These differences can certainly generate tensions, too. As you go through work, and through life, of course you're going to have feelings. Clearing the air by expressing yourself honestly is good, but doing it with anger or by personal attack is not only unnecessary but destructive. Anger causes emotional *flooding* in the other person, a sense of being overwhelmed by feelings that are difficult to control. People grow fearful. Their commitment to the group process and to the person who is showing anger becomes shaken.

Skillful leaders avoid rage and contempt like the plague. A leader cannot afford to be controlled by negative emotions. People with Leadership Character take responsibility for creating the positive mood that leads to a culture of respect and creative results, whether they are in formal positions of authority or not.

Much of leadership is about managing emotion in others. As discussed in chapter 3, people in a group catch emotions from one another, especially from their leaders, on whom most attention is focused. If the leader can't maintain positive emotions, the group won't either. When a leader acts negatively and angrily, whether in overt, abusive ways, as Steve did, or in more subtly undermining ways, as Jamal did, everyone is infected by those emotions. The attitudes displayed by the leader deeply influence the tenor of the group.

Managing emotions is also essential to another aspect of leadership: clear thinking. Well-documented research into stress shows that when a person's thinking is clouded by anger or anxiety, the primitive fight-or-flight response kicks in. Blood is diverted from the brain to the limbs for motion, and it's literally less possible to think clearly. It's easy for emotions to overwhelm intellect when the brain isn't getting enough oxygen. You can be swept away by anger or anxiety, but clear thinking is critical to alert, responsive leadership, whether you're leading a neighborhood association meeting, a team designing a manufacturing process, or a Fortune 500 company.

The best leaders' skills of empathy allow them to do just what a deft psychologist is able to do when working with people who are in great emotional pain. You might say, "I wouldn't want that high degree of empathy because I just can't be objective. I'm afraid I'd lose distance, and it would be too hard on me to experience other people's pain." As you discovered in chapter 2, however, the various components of Leadership Character are complementary, and this is where emotional mastery comes into play. Emotional mastery gives you the resilience to handle anything that comes your way. So rather than avoiding other people's intense feelings because of the fear that they might make you uncomfortable, your goal should be to recognize and honor what people are experiencing while modulating the way you experience it yourself. Being empathetic and mastering emotions are the challenges of an excellent therapist, and also of an excellent leader.

Thinking Past Your Emotions

When our son Rob was quite young, Bob made a point of talking with him about how important it is to stay calm in an emergency and not to panic, so that you can think calmly and clearly. Bob told Rob to stay "calm, cool, and collected" if he were ever in a crisis.

One day when Rob was about 5 years old, Lyn was driving him to a kindergarten event. "I was rounding a corner in the neighborhood—going slowly, thankfully—when I heard Rob say, "Mom, stop the car. I'm falling out." Lyn looked over her shoulder and saw Rob partially out of the car, his hands clinging to an open door. She stopped the car and Rob climbed back in, unhurt. He seemed amazingly calm, and they just continued on their way.

When Bob came home, Rob went running to him, shouting. "Dad, you saved my life today! I was riding in the car with Mom and when my door came open and I was falling out I just thought: 'Calm, cool, and collected,' over and over. And I told Mom to stop the car, and I was okay." Because Rob was mentally prepared at such a young age, even in that simple way, to recognize and set aside the feelings of panic and confusion that normally would have gripped a child in that predicament, he avoided a potentially serious and life-altering injury.

Mastering powerful feelings like fear and anger requires you to develop a keen awareness of your emotions and the way they affect you and others. It also means developing the ability to change and adapt those emotions by changing your thinking. You must recognize that internal emotional reactions are not automatic; they are mediated by your attitudes and thoughts. Developing emotional mastery comes down to learning how to monitor and manage your thoughts, attitudes, and emotions, and the behavior that results from them. You monitor thoughts and emotions through self-awareness. You change them through conducting an inner dialogue, which we refer to as *self-talk*.

Effective Self-Management (ESM) is a method for reaching the goal of emotional mastery. It provides a model for understanding human emotions and for developing the emotional responses that are most useful to you. Besides helping you eliminate unnecessary negative emotions, it is a method that can aid in the development of attitudes and skills that will increase confidence and make your interpersonal relationships more productive. It will help you improve how you function in organizations and be more effective in handling challenges in all parts of your life. In fact, applying the skill of emotional mastery in personal relationships often has a positive effect on performance in your career, as the elimination of excessive tension from whatever source releases more energy for accomplishing things at work.

Building on the ideas of Albert Ellis, a pioneering behaviorist, Maxie Maultsby, a psychiatrist at the University of Kentucky, developed a model for increasing personal effectiveness called Rational Behavior Training.[2] Effective Self-Management is modeled closely on the principles of Rational Behavior Training. The central idea of ESM is that outside events or other people don't cause our emotions. Rather, our emotions are the result of how we think and talk to ourselves about these things outside ourselves.

When we experience or witness an external event, by hearing another person speak or observing an interaction between two other people, for example, our eyes and ears send nerve impulses to the neocortex, the thinking part of the brain. The neocortex in turn translates these impulses into images. The brain then evaluates these images as positive, negative, or neutral, filtering them through attitudes, or preconceptions, or habitual responses we may have in place, and then generates a sequence of thoughts about them. The neocortex is tied to the limbic system, the feeling part of the brain. The emotional responses, that is, the physiological changes that we call our feelings or emotions, will be those that correlate with the thoughts we have had.

For example, let's assume that two people in management positions, John and Jane, hear Tom, their manager, give a presentation on a proposed reorganization of top management. John is given more responsibility but a less prestigious title and his reaction is negative. He is fuming when he gets home, and he tells his wife, "That was a stupid, unworkable plan. Tom infuriates me." Jane's position, on the other hand, is upgraded by the new plan and she feels elated. "I was so happy to hear Tom say that," she tells a co-worker. "That meeting really made me feel good." Obviously

FIGURE 2: **Effective Self-Management (ESM)**

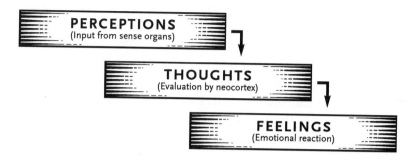

Tom's presentation didn't cause John's or Jane's emotions; their feelings were caused by how they evaluated, or thought about, the event. The input was identical: both heard the same speech. Their thinking about the speech, though, was very different, and their different thoughts produced different feelings.

The sequence, then, leading from external event to emotional reaction, is shown in Figure 2.

THOUGHT MEDIATES FEELINGS

Jamal's Story

When our habitual self-talk is so deeply ingrained that we aren't even aware of it, the emotions it can produce seem perfectly natural. Here is how Jamal (the manufacturing VP who was passed over for the presidency of his corporate unit) remembers reacting at that time.

"I felt undervalued. I felt righteous indignation, and that was something I had felt often in other situations. When you're in a company for 25 years, of course you will have some setbacks. In my case, I usually took them personally and felt victimized."

Of his executive development program experience, Jamal says, "The first thing that struck me as helpful was gaining the understanding of how you're always dealing with myriad personalities: my peers, the people that work for me, my boss. . . . In my narrow viewpoint I used to think, 'Here's the goal and we're all going for it, so why are we having so much conflict?' I gained an appreciation for the different ways individuals accomplish similar goals."

One day, in a coaching session, Jamal had what he now calls "a true *aha!*" experience. Bob was illustrating the idea of monitoring and managing thinking as the way to achieve emotional mastery. "Bob asked me to think of the kinds of things people might say to me at work that would make me want to just leap over the table and choke them," Jamal remembers. Then Bob told Jamal, "Now imagine you're going to visit a dear friend who's had a breakdown, in a psychiatric hospital. Imagine that while you're riding the elevator up to his room, another patient blurts out the very same thing that would have made you so angry. What would you want to do then? Choke her?" Jamal immediately said, "No, of course not. I'd want to calm her down. She's sick." And Bob said, "You've just proved that it's within you to respond in a way that's more productive." Jamal went on to say, "At that moment, right in Bob's office, I suddenly felt like I was watching a videotape of my life, rewinding all the way back to when I was a kid. Case after case of reacting to things with righteous indignation, feeling like a victim. And, not just me, but my mother, and some of my relatives. And me with my children. I remembered a whole host of experiences that were the same symptomatic, knee-jerk way of reacting to situations, when I would just think, 'How could they *do* that to me? How could they *do* that to my kid?'"

• • •

Reframing Emotional Responses

ESM teaches people to alter emotional reactions, but the goal is not the suppression of feelings. Recognition and expression of feelings are vital for a relaxed, well-functioning body. When your thoughts about a situation arouse anger, it is not wise simply to

——

deny the emotion and avoid expressing it. If you wish to decrease the amount of anger felt, it is your attitude toward the situation that must be changed.

Neither is it necessary or useful to eliminate all "negative" emotions. It is the *degree* of emotion that is of concern. For example, if an employee you supervise is consistently performing below standard, some degree of irritation and tension is probably necessary to keep you sufficiently focused on the problem to work out a solution. Extreme anger, however, decreases clarity of thought, alters optimal physiological functioning, and is unpleasant to experience both for you and for the people around you.

Effective Self-Management works by teaching people to alter their thinking patterns in ways that will result in more satisfactory emotional responses by using more realistic, and usually more positive, self-talk.

Imagine the thoughts of a typical parent whose teenage son is an hour late getting home. "Why isn't he here? He could at least have called. He may have totaled the car and be on his way to a hospital now! If he hasn't had a wreck and is just fooling around somewhere, I'll really give him a piece of my mind. I might as well stay up and wait—how could I sleep in this state?" The feelings that naturally follow such thoughts are fear, anxiety, and anger.

But consider the difference when the parent substitutes a calmer, more realistic self-talk in the same situation. "Well, he's late, but I have no way of knowing why. So I may as well not waste time worrying about it. Besides, it's really not likely that anything tragic has happened. I'll go to bed and set the alarm for two o'clock. If he's not here by then, maybe there will be cause for alarm and I can call the police and the hospitals then." The emotional reaction now is concern, not debilitating anxiety and anger.

A key component of this process is to work toward maintaining those emotional responses that are goal producing. Before deciding on the thoughts and feelings you wish to have, it is necessary to clearly define your goals and values. For the parent whose son was late coming home, we can assume that the parent's primary goals in the situation were to:

- Protect the son

- Get the necessary rest

- Make sure the situation did not repeat itself

Anger and anxiety were not necessary for satisfying any of these goals. In order for the parent to be able to rest, in fact, negative emotions had to be kept at a minimum. A certain level of emotion was necessary for meeting the first and third goals, but to protect the son, concern was more in order than extreme anxiety. Some degree of irritation would have been useful for reminding the parent to talk to the son about not staying out too late again.

With Effective Self-Management, then, rather than blocking our emotions, we use *reframing* of our thinking to realistically decrease the intensity and frequency of negative emotions, and to increase the intensity and frequency of positive ones.

RATIONAL THINKING

According to Dr. Maultsby, thinking is rational when it

- Is based on objective reality

- Helps you protect your life

- Is goal producing

- Prevents significant emotional conflict

- Prevents significant conflict with others

These five criteria provide a guide that you can deliberately use in Effective Self-Management to decide whether or not a specific thought, feeling, or action is rational and in your own best interest.

For example, imagine that John says his supervisor makes him angry because he requires John to work late. If John believes that other people's actions are the cause of his feelings, it seems natural to him to get angry at his supervisor for this, even though he may not like feeling that way. So it would be useful for John if he had a way to decide when his thinking is rational, or in his best interest, and when it is not.

John should be able to see that the idea that his supervisor makes him angry is not based on objective reality. John makes himself angry by taking the view he does of his supervisor's request. In fact, when he thinks about it, John will remember that he has often worked late without thinking twice. He is upsetting himself now because working late interferes with a planned family outing.

John next asks himself if getting angry is goal producing. Obviously, his anger is counterproductive; it's unlikely that getting mad will influence his supervisor to let him leave early. A calm discussion of the situation has more chance of success.

He can also ask himself, "Is this thought causing me significant emotional conflict?" For most people anger is an extremely negative feeling, and John may well decide that feeling this angry amounts to significant emotional conflict for him. He already must deal with the possibility of missing the family trip. Why add the distress of an angry reaction to an already bad situation?

John also assesses whether his thinking might cause unwanted conflict with his supervisor. Doesn't it seem more likely that the relationship will go the way John wants it to if he remains calm, thus increasing his ability to discuss the problem with the supervisor?

John, then, may decide that his thinking doesn't meet four of the five criteria. The second criterion, "Helps you protect your life," is probably irrelevant in this situation, although getting angry often over time has been found to be associated with certain physiological disorders that could actually shorten one's life.

The fourth and fifth criteria contain the word *significant*, which is a variable and subjective quality. Part of learning emotional mastery is becoming aware of your own limits: how you do and do not want to feel. Such self-knowledge is what enables you to tailor these criteria to yourself and use them as guides to assess the situations that come up every day. People simply differ in the amount of conflict and unpleasant feelings they find tolerable. A politician, for example, endures considerable conflict in campaigning, and it's no secret that election to office involves plenty of challenge and conflict. Encountering it shouldn't cause a person to withdraw from the race. In any case, most people drawn to running for office have a high tolerance for stress. Fortunately for most of us, who have a lower tolerance for it, most career paths require far less conflict.

Challenging Perceptions with Rational Self-Analysis

One unusual feature of Dr. Maultsby's technique is its use of a specific, written method for determining if our thoughts and actions are rational. This method, called Rational Self-Analysis (RSA), involves checking, or challenging, each of our perceptions and thoughts about a situation. We use, as tools for challenging ourselves, the five criteria of rational thinking just discussed.

RSA is divided into five steps:

1. Situation

2. Thoughts about the situation

3. Feelings

4. Challenges to thoughts

5. Emotional goals for the future

You start with step 1, describing the situation. Here's an example: "I don't like my co-worker Janice. She's always late and never does her share of the work." Before going further, do a *camera check* of your statement. Ask yourself, "If a camera took a picture of this situation, would it correspond to the facts I have stated?" Possibly not, even in our simple example. Words like *always* and *never* are risky, for instance. It's unlikely that anyone is *always* late or *never* does her share of the work.

Thoughts about the situation follow in step 2. In this case, your thoughts might be:

———

- "I can't stand it when she comes in late."

- "It's unfair that she can come in late and do so little work but get paid the same as I do."

- "It's terrible for her to behave that way. She's a pain in the neck."

- "Janice really makes me mad."

In step 3, you list the feelings, such as anger and resentment, that this kind of thinking generates. Then in step 4, challenge your step 2 thoughts by saying:

- "The reality of the situation is that I *can* stand for her to come in late; I have been working with her for a year and nothing has happened to me because of it yet. Saying I can't stand it only makes me feel more angry. It would be more accurate to simply say that I don't like it."

- "It would be nice if the world were fair, and I can wish that it were. I can try to make it more fair, but simply demanding fairness and upsetting myself because a situation is not fair gets me nowhere. A demand for fairness is definitely irrational because it violates objective reality, is not goal producing, and causes me significant internal conflict. Furthermore, there is no real reason for me to expect Janice's behavior to be like mine. If I am willing to accept the possible consequences, I can also come in late and do less work. Actually, I'm getting less done anyway because I'm expending all this energy in anger at her."

- "It may be unfortunate that I work with someone who doesn't live up to what I think are proper work standards, but it is not terrible. I am not her supervisor and can do little to alter the situation other than to request a transfer to another department. Certainly she is not literally a pain in the neck, although I do usually wind up with a headache and an uncomfortable stomach at the end of the day. These, however, are probably physiological expressions of anger and resentment that result from my negative thoughts about her. If I am going to stay in the department, it would be much better to simply say that this is an unfortunate situation that really has little to do with me."

- "Obviously, this statement is untrue because it violates the first criterion. She can't make me mad; I choose to upset myself because of the view I take of her behavior."

In step 5, you might list emotional goals such as:

- "I would like to feel no more than mild annoyance when Janice behaves in ways that I don't like."

- "I would like to remain calm during work hours so that I can more easily complete my job assignments and can feel better when I get home."

It's clear from this example, too, that the language you use to describe a situation has a dramatic effect on your reaction. How many times have you heard people say things like, "I feel trapped," or "This job is killing me," or "She just makes my blood boil," or, "If he says that one more time I'm going to scream." Extreme metaphors like these intensify emotional reactions. Simply saying, "I don't like this situation because . . ." or "I don't like his behavior because . . ." elicits a much calmer reaction and allows you to focus on the sources of your displeasure and possibly do something about them.

Changing Entrenched Emotional Reactions

Some emotional reactions can be altered quickly simply by using Rational Self-Analysis and a more positive and objective self-talk; others require a great deal more effort. There are some situations in which the person is not aware of negative self-talk but still experiences negative emotions. That was certainly the situation with Jamal, who had unconsciously been in the habit of seeing himself as a victim ever since his childhood.

In these cases we usually find that an unexpressed attitude accounts for the reaction. For example, if Jack grew up with a mother who constantly told him how dangerous thunderstorms were and who screamed with every lightning bolt, it is highly likely that a thunderstorm will evoke a strong fear reaction. He does not have to tell himself how terribly dangerous thunderstorms are; each time one occurs the reaction appears spontaneously. We say that he has developed an entrenched attitude about storms.

Changing this type of undesirable emotional reaction requires first uncovering the underlying self-talk responsible for the attitude. We begin by asking the question, "He is behaving as if he believed what?" In this example, Jack is behaving as if he believed that thunderstorms are terribly dangerous and that he will probably be hurt by a storm, but the reality of the situation is that although thunderstorms can be dangerous, they usually are not. Jack is a victim of a common error: he is basing his behavior on remote possibilities rather than on actual probabilities.

To change such an unwanted fear reaction, Jack would first write out a more realistic self-talk to be used in the situation. He might write,

> *Even though thunderstorms can be dangerous, the fact is that I have known very few people who have been hurt by them. Furthermore, because I can do little to avoid being hurt by one outside of avoiding trees and taking cover, my intense fear serves no purpose. I might as well remain calm and not dwell on the remote possibility that I might be hurt. Besides, riding in a car is actually much more dangerous, and I am able to do that quite calmly every day.*

Just substituting this self-talk will probably serve to lessen the intensity of the emotional reactions, but a fear reaction will probably still occur during a storm. Because the situation has been paired with a feeling of fear so many times, Jack has been strongly conditioned to behave this way. This kind of automatic pairing of situation and feeling occurs frequently.

In addition to a more positive self-talk, a technique called Rational Emotive Imagery (REI) can be used to hasten the process of uncoupling a situation from a feeling you have learned to let it evoke. The first step in this visualization technique is to relax completely. You can accomplish this through deep-breathing exercises, meditation, or yoga stretching. After you're in a relaxed state, you visualize the total sequence of events normally occurring in the situation, maintaining at all times the desired emotional state. If at any point undesired feelings like tension, anger, or anxiety are aroused, interrupt the process and repeat the relaxation exercise.

After relaxing, Jack would visualize an entire thunderstorm, seeing each lightning bolt and hearing every thunderclap, without letting himself react anxiously. Learning any new behavior—or unlearning an old one—requires practice, and doing Rational Emotive Imagery provides an opportunity for practice even though the actual situation is not available. Relearning might be much slower if Jack had to wait for real thunderstorms to practice his desired reaction. REI is a technique you can use to speed the process.

REDUCING ANGER AND GROWING AS A LEADER

Steve's Story

Anger is one of the most troublesome emotions in our culture. We are taught many conflicting ideas about anger. Some say, "You shouldn't get angry;" others, "You should always express your anger;" and others, "It's okay to get angry, but don't let anyone know it, especially at work." Effective Self-Management does not teach suppression of anger. It does, however, teach you to experience only that amount of anger that is sufficient to aid you in reaching your goals.

Most people agree that anger is an unpleasant emotion to feel, and most of us would like to reduce its frequency and intensity. Changing your reaction first requires recognizing that you are the cause of your own anger. Only when you see yourself as the cause of your feelings will you accept responsibility for changing them. This recognition alone can go a long way toward tempering your anger.

Steve, for example, that volatile software company VP who was experienced by his co-workers as a bully, now believes that his "challenge was a fundamental trust issue. I did not recognize any special talent *in myself.* I thought my success could just be attributed to desire and effort." Inevitably, this colored how he saw those he worked with. "I did not trust other people to do their best. I felt that if they only worked harder and cared more, they would have greater success."

Steve's work on his emotional mastery brought him to recognize that only he himself was answerable for his outbursts. He began to change things at work by apologizing to those he had offended and making it clear to each of them that he was taking full responsibility for making the relationships work.

We asked Steve to make a point of praising his people and to refrain from any criticism for one month. "I had no idea of the tremendous value of praise," he says now. "I was totally surprised at how much people want to please, how much they value approval and how much they respond to praise." We also asked him to meet at least once a week, separately, with each person to ask for input, advice, or suggestions for improving the business, and to work with them to implement as many of these ideas as possible.

Above all, Steve worked hardest to reframe his thinking so that he could control his emotions. When someone did things that he thought were stupid, instead of saying to himself, "I can't believe what an idiot he is," and exploding, he would deliberately think, "This person is fallible and lacks either the information or the experience to handle this challenge well. I'll have to figure out what I can do to see that this doesn't happen again."

Steve's whole idea of what he does has been transformed. "Today, I am more focused on leadership than on management," he says. "I take a more balanced view between the means and the end. I weigh more heavily the impact on people of reaching an objective. I am more patient and tend to work through the organization rather than going around it when something is not working. I work to achieve consensus. I try to frame expectations that we all agree on.

"That's a challenge for me. I work with some strong-willed, highly successful people. I also work with some people who are much less talented. Achieving consensus can result in things being pulled down. I am still demanding, but today I understand so much more about the needs of the people I work with, and how to nurture and respond to them."

In his current job as president of a sports clothing company, Steve gives this as an illustration: "Today, I honor the project plans of my direct reports. I realize that if I impose my changes on their engagements and initiatives, they will not hesitate to let the project become my responsibility. The implications are that I have to prepare the staff before they make their plans; I cannot change their plans with impunity after the fact. Further, I no longer commit to my peers or the board before knowing what the commitment is from the staff and then try to force compliance, which I often did as a manager."

• • •

Emotional Mastery Is a Process

Achieving mastery over a volatile emotion such as anger can seem like an impossibly big task, but as with any other goal worth aiming for, reaching it is a matter of taking the first small action, and then taking all the necessary successive small actions after that. Emotional mastery is a process. As you get started, it's a good idea to do a complete Rational Self-Analysis on each situation you encounter that results in excessive anger, going step by step, as described. As Steve soon found, though, more positive thoughts should start to come to you naturally in such situations, and you will not need to go through the RSA process continually. Of course, if similar situations or patterns have elicited anger in you for a very long time, your reaction may be more firmly entrenched. Rational Emotive Imagery, described earlier, can help to interrupt the pattern.

But like every aspect of Leadership Character, emotional mastery is more a goal to constantly strive for than a state of perfection to attain once and for all. "I know that I have to work on practicing these principles of emotional maturity," says Jamal, who used to get angry because he saw himself as a victim. "It's not something that comes naturally to me. But working on it has made a difference, and not just at work, but in the situations I encounter on a day-to-day basis in my personal life. About a year after I started working with this process, I asked my wife if she had noticed anything different about me as a result. She said, 'In the past year you have not cursed. Every time we used to come to a traffic light that had just turned, or when someone cut you off, or something didn't go right for you, the first words out of your mouth used to be a curse.' I have a different way of dealing with anger now. I don't react the same way at all."

Key Concepts

- Emotional mastery is essential for clear thinking and for creating a culture of respect; effective leaders are effective masters of their emotions.

- Achieving emotional mastery depends on controlling the size and nature of your negative emotions. It helps to remember that trust and respect take years to build but only a moment to destroy.

- Mastering emotions is possible through an ongoing process of changing the way you talk to yourself and the way you frame your emotional responses.

5

Lack of Blame

G o into any company and interview people at random about their jobs. What are the challenges they feel? What frustrates them? From almost everyone, you will hear stories that hinge on blame, either of another department, another person, or some external situation.

It seems that when things aren't going smoothly, blame is a natural human response. Reacting with anger is the quick, easy thing to do. But when we give in to blame, we are unwittingly confusing a central element of responsible behavior—that people should be accountable for what they do—with the notion that people should be accused and faulted when what they do is problematic. Blame goes beyond accountability and easily bleeds into looking for a scapegoat. It's the easy way out when something goes wrong. It's true that handling problem situations in ways that avoid blame is harder; it requires us to think more creatively, and not to lose perspective. The ultimate task of decent people and good leaders, though, is to model accountability in our own behavior and thereby elicit it from others. There are also practical reasons to insist on accountability without blaming: blame is simply a poor motivator, and an incredible waste of time.

In the mid-1970s, Bob worked as chief psychologist and director of children's services at a community mental health center. His boss was capricious and unfair and frequently lost his composure and got angry at the staff. Bob and his colleagues spent a lot of time talking about how horrible the situation was, blaming the boss for his behavior. Those colleagues spent a lot of time at Bob and Lyn's house, so Lyn heard all the complaints, too.

"I listened to all the stories and got angrier and angrier," Lyn remembers. "It was hard for me to see Bob and our friends in such a tough situation. I was at home with Rob, who was a toddler at the time, and found myself spending much of the day thinking about how bad Bob's boss was: composing mental letters to him, even fantasizing about revenge." In a short time, Bob chose to leave this organization. A few years later we heard that the former boss was in a nursing home with a degenerative neurological disease, so he had almost certainly been unable to control his bad behavior.

For whatever reasons, it was clear that this man had poor emotional mastery, and so did the rest of us for spending so much of our time getting upset. None of us had the ability to change the situation or the boss, but we each had a choice about how we reacted. Choosing to blame the boss only led to continual emotional upset for all of us, day after day. We believed at the time that it was he who was causing our anger, but in reality we were doing this to ourselves.

BLAME VS. RESPECT AND RESPONSIBILITY

Chris Argyris is a brilliant academician in the field of organization behavior and a proponent of constantly challenging your own assumptions. In the article "Teaching Smart People How to Learn," Argyris uses an example that strikes close to home. He describes a team of consultants who had completed a project that had not gone well. In debriefing the project, they spent all their time discussing how uncooperative the client was, and how troubled the organization was. They were blaming the client instead of asking what they, as consultants, could have done differently to make the project a success. Argyris says that it's easy for all of us to look outward rather than inward when something has gone wrong. Moreover, he points out, blame comes especially easily to successful people. They use blame and defensive reasoning to avoid responsibility and real learning. He writes:

> *Put simply, because many professionals are almost always successful at what they do, they rarely experience failure. And because they have rarely failed, they have never learned how to learn from failure. So whenever their single-loop learning strategies go wrong, they become defensive, screen out criticism, and put the "blame" on anyone and everyone but themselves. In short, their ability to learn shuts down precisely at the moment they need it most.*[1]

A similar point is made in the Arbinger Institute's *Leadership and Self Deception*, a book that reinforces the fact that leadership can't be developed without developing who we are.[2] Core to its premise is the fact that we often look outside ourselves, blaming others and leading in an egocentric and self-centered way rather than in an honest, ethical, genuine way that serves the organization.

So, convinced of the damaging effects of blame on personal responsibility, we placed blame on the responsibility side of the scale in the earlier version of the Leadership Character Model. If you give yourself the out of blaming others, you will never take real responsibility yourself. It's true of the customer who sues a restaurant because she spills coffee in her lap, and of the marketing VP who blames the sales department for a quarter's bad numbers. The key movement in anyone's development from adolescence to adulthood is from blaming others to taking personal responsibility.

Over time, as we analyzed how people were rated by others on 360-degree reviews, it became evident that scores on those measures that relate to lack of blame tended to correlate quite closely with scores on other indicators of respect, and less closely with scores on responsibility. In a factor analysis of our data, lack of blame clustered with empathy, emotional mastery, and humility. Striving to find the clearest way to explain the qualities of character essential for authentic, integrity-based leadership, we concluded that lack of blame is best seen as a central quality of respectful relationships, so we shifted it to the respect side of the scale.

Blame not only destroys a culture of mutual respect; it destroys a culture of personal responsibility. As we've said before, there is a fluid interplay among all the qualities of character; developing your skills in any of the components of Leadership Character can help you enhance your abilities in the others. In fact, it's rather difficult to improve in one *without* naturally developing in others. For one thing, letting go of the habit of blaming others for problems requires you to master emotions such as anger and impatience. If you want to understand why people make mistakes you will have to consider other people with empathy, and be able to support them in positive change. It will take a strong sense of accountability and a heavy dose of humility to be able to look at yourself or your organization first when something goes wrong. We are not saying that you should shift blame from others to yourself. Rather, we encourage you to focus on solutions instead of blame.

SPURRING GROWTH WITH UNDERSTANDING

We certainly are familiar with the impulse to blame, because we've felt it ourselves. One day when our younger son, Josh, was about eight years old, Bob saw him crying on his way home from the school bus stop. Josh was reluctant to say what was wrong but finally admitted that an older kid had been bullying him, and that this had been going on for some time. "I was angry," Bob recalls. "My first instinct was to call the other boy's parents, go to their house, sit them all down, and 'read the bully the riot act.' But then I thought, 'What would Ken Kelley have done?'"

Ken Kelley was Bob's close friend from elementary through high school. He was a natural leader from a very young age. "I can't remember one instance when Ken blamed others. If he had an issue, he would just put it on the table in a respectful way." Once several of Ken's friends were bullying another student. Ken went to each one of them, asked how he would feel if someone treated him that way, and described how he himself would have felt to be the target. The bullying stopped. This kind of decency and directness made other kids react to Ken as a leader. He encouraged empathy rather than reacting with blame.

People like Ken, who handle things without blame, gain tremendous "referent power." They can influence others even in the absence of any formal authority. People just want to follow them out of respect, and, interestingly, people with strong referent power seldom abuse it. Ken died in a helicopter crash during the Vietnam War. "To this day," Bob says, "I believe that Ken would have been our country's president if he had not died. He has always lived on in my memory as a role model. Even all those years later when I confronted this dilemma of seeing my child bullied, the memory of Ken helped me find a better solution than blame."

From Rob, our older son, Bob learned that the child who had been bullying Josh, whom we'll call Cal, had been in trouble with the juvenile courts, and that his best friend had just been placed in a detention center for breaking into a home. Rob also mentioned that Cal rode his bike on our street quite often. So the next day, Bob made sure he was working in the front yard when Cal came along. Here's what happened:

"I put my hand out to stop the boy and said, 'Cal, I heard that your friend got into trouble. I know you must feel bad about it. You probably tried to talk him out of breaking into that house.' Cal said, 'Yeah, I tried to tell him not to do it, but he wouldn't listen.' I thought it just as likely that Cal had actually been with his friend and simply had not been caught, but I continued to talk with him, saying things that would make him feel good about himself. I purposely never mentioned his bullying of Josh. Every day after that Cal would ride his bike by our house and greet me. He never bullied Josh again."

If Bob had approached Cal's family with anger and blame as he first felt like doing, he probably could have ended the bullying of Josh. Cal would have been afraid of provoking Bob's anger another time, but Cal most likely would have been punished by his parents and later would have taken it out on some other smaller child. Eliminating blame, considering what was behind the bad behavior, and reframing the experience was a more creative approach. It not only solved the immediate problem but perhaps also helped a troubled child choose behavior that could make him a better person.

DRIVING A WEDGE WITH BLAME

When there is a problem, of course you want to resolve it, and it's likely that the troublesome situation did result at least in part from mistakes people made. So when you react by assigning blame you may feel that you are justified in letting off steam and that you are just emphatically letting the responsible parties know they are at fault. But blame usually backfires. Not only can blaming others make it harder to resolve the immediate issue; it creates a lasting unproductive dynamic in your relationships. Most important, though, it takes the heat off of you. When you blame others, you defend yourself, and your own personal responsibility in the situation gets easily lost.

We often see people not accepting responsibility and instead blaming upper management: "If they would just give us good direction, keep us informed . . . we'd be okay." But the minute employees start blaming their bosses, they stop thinking about what needs to be done to solve a problem. People with Leadership Character, no matter where they are in an organization, say, "What can I do?" not "Who's at fault here?"

Conflict, open but constructive, is a necessary and useful part of the life of any organization, but that conflict is most helpful if it is about tasks: "How should we market this service?" or, "What's the best way to recover with this customer?" However, where there is a culture of blame and a focus on who did what rather than on problem solving, the conflict becomes a personality conflict, which can be terribly destructive.

———

Although they may not show it outwardly, when people feel blamed they often react with anger and hurt feelings and begin defending themselves. If they feel blamed by someone who is in a position of power over them, these reactions can be even more pronounced. They ruminate over the experience; the embarrassment, humiliation, and sense of unfairness loom larger and larger. In time, the original problem can come to take second place in their minds to their raw feelings and rationalization. So as their leader, you have defeated your own immediate purpose of fixing the error. You have set up a situation in which the person who should be putting effort into understanding what went wrong and resolving things is instead spending time and energy nursing hurt feelings.

That is the short-term consequence, but the long-term effect is even more disturbing. Assigning blame creates distance between you and other people, making it more rather than less likely that problems will recur. If you're a manager, it makes people less likely to report concerns or potential problems—often until they blow up in your face. On their part, fearing blame, people have a harder time facing mistakes honestly and thus are less likely to learn from them and more prone to repeat them. On your part, if you're putting energy into assigning fault, you're not putting energy into sorting out what went wrong. Over time, you may also find yourself in the awkward position of trying to function, or lead, while important information is withheld from you. If people fear that the messenger with bad news will be shot, then that is a role they will shun. Problems can easily be compounded before you ever realize their existence.

THE FEELING WAS MUTUAL

Truc's Story

Problems in a relationship are rarely caused by the behavior of just one side or the other, but we often make the problems much worse by focusing only on the faults and errors of the other person. In the internal drama played in our heads, we are the perfect person and the other person is doing things we dislike, treating us in ways we find objectionable. Breaking the habit of blaming means accepting the fact that we are all highly fallible human beings, capable of making mistakes and doing things wrong. Learning that helped Truc develop his Leadership Character.

Truc was a regional sales director for a firm in the consumer package goods industry. "The relationships I had with the people reporting to me were excellent," he remembers. "But the relationship I had with the person I reported to was crumbling." Truc's immediate boss, the person who had hired him years before, had recently been demoted. "He was hurt," Truc recalls. "He was basically saying, 'I will show them they were wrong.' So he made demands on us that were unrealistic. At one point, I had a stack of papers maybe 18 inches high. 'These are the things that you're asking my people to do,' I told him. 'They can't do all this and do their own jobs, too.' He said, 'You just don't understand.' And so I held the papers up chest high, dropped them on his office floor, and said, '*You* sort it out.' I wasn't very good at politics," he ruefully recalls now.

Around this time Truc joined our executive development program. When he received his 360-degree review, his peers and direct reports gave him rave reviews, but as you might expect, his boss scored him significantly lower. It was clear that Truc felt blamed by his boss. In discussing the boss's behavior, Truc said his response was to avoid him, be around him as little as possible, and just continue trying to do his own job well.

It seemed obvious that Truc's boss would feel blamed, too, on top of whatever bad feelings he had from his recent demotion. To test this hypothesis, Bob asked Truc to try re-engaging with his boss—to not avoid him for two weeks. He asked Truc to look for things the boss did well and comment on them through email, notes, or voice mail, or person to person. He was to focus especially on things the boss did well as a leader. Within a week, Truc called excitedly to say that he and his boss were like old friends again and that they had scheduled several trips together to visit their top clients around the country.

—

"There were certainly mistakes being made above me," Truc says now, "but there was also self-revelation—that some of these mistakes could have been caused by me. It wasn't just somebody else's fault." Truc also learned that he could have an effect on those above him. "It's easy to manage down because you're in a position of strength, but managing up is not something I would ever have thought of. It was a like a light bulb going on in my head: this guy I was reporting to has got a lot of pressures on him, so why don't I try to get my way by trying to understand what he's going through—coaching him without his even knowing?"

Truc's story shows how mutual blame can cause big problems, and it also reveals the intimate connections between getting beyond blame and strengthening other elements of Leadership Character like empathy, emotional mastery, and focusing on the whole. "Maybe you're given something to do that you don't like," Truc says, "but you see it's worthwhile to the business. You can say, 'It's going to be a lot of work, but I understand where you're coming from and why I have to do that.' More than anything, I learned the importance of trying to understand what makes the people I'm interacting with think, and that different people think differently."

• • •

UNDERMINING LEADERSHIP WITH A BLAMING STYLE

Scholars of organizational psychology describe six styles of leadership. First identified by Harvard University psychologist David McClelland[3] and others, and later refined by other scholars, including Daniel Goleman and his colleagues, these styles are affiliative, coaching, coercive (or commanding), visionary (or authoritative), democratic (or participative), and pacesetting.[4] One or another style may predominate in any individual leader's behavior, but Goleman has pointed out that the best results come when a leader can switch seamlessly among them and use them purposefully to meet the challenges of varying situations.

The coercive and pacesetting styles of leadership rely heavily, and unproductively for the most part, on blame. A pacesetting leader doesn't want to be bothered with explaining things. She sets a high bar and insists that both she and her subordinates hurdle it. When they don't, or can't, she is eager to criticize, and to replace them. Goleman observes that this style can "get quick results from a highly motivated and competent team."[5] But because it relies on an attitude of blame, and because motivation and competency are very often not present, it more often has a negative impact on the functioning of the organization and disturbing effects on morale. "The pacesetting style destroys climate," Goleman writes. "Work becomes not a matter of doing one's best along a clear course so much as second-guessing what the leader wants. At the same time, people often feel that the pacesetter doesn't trust them to work in their own way or to take initiative. . . . The pacesetter either gives no feedback on how people are doing or jumps in to take over when she thinks they're lagging."[6]

Coercive leaders want to give orders and see them followed immediately. There are crisis moments, or times when a turnaround needs to be kick-started, when this approach is useful, but it, too, has disastrous effects on organizational climate. "The leader's extreme top-down decision making kills new ideas on the vine. People feel so disrespected that they think, 'I won't even bring my ideas up; they'll only be shot down.' Likewise, people's sense of responsibility evaporates: unable to act on their own initiative, they lose their sense of ownership and feel little accountability for their performance."[7]

The drawbacks of these styles of leadership are even clearer when we consider that, according to Goleman's analysis, climate accounts for nearly a third of business results.[8] There are times when the strategic application of a pacesetting or coercive style can be valuable, but leaders who rely on them are people who need to recognize the generally negative effects of blame. Contrast those styles with affiliative leadership, which, as Goleman describes it, doesn't rely on blame but instead illustrates empathy in action.

Affiliative leaders "expand the connective tissue with the people they lead," he writes.[9] "This focus makes empathy—the ability to sense the feelings, needs, and perspectives of others—another fundamental competence here."[10] Goleman describes the affiliative style as an "all-weather resonance builder." You can imagine the positive effects this style has on climate. The most effective leaders, who are able to switch successfully among the various styles depending on what a situation calls for, says Goleman, "are exquisitely sensitive to the impact they are having on others." They are, in other words, strong in all the core qualities of respect.

A PACESETTING LEADER LEARNS BALANCE

Jim's Story

Truc's problems with blame were mainly directed upward, but Jim was the classic pacesetter: a hard-charging, results-driven leader who had no time for the problems of those unfortunate enough to find themselves below him in the hierarchy.

At a major utility company, Jim had reached a plateau that he couldn't seem to get beyond, doing executive support work. "I was doing officer-level work," he says, "but I came to the realization that I was not eligible to be an officer, though it wasn't clear to me why." So he left, taking an opportunity to help a friend who had a company (that had been losing money) providing contract services to the telephone industry.

Within a few months, Jim had increased sales and started the firm on a path of rapid growth. "I was combining the roles of CEO, COO, and CFO and doing some sales work, too," he explains. He ran a lean-and-mean organization. "We had only a small internal salaried staff. Most of our employees were external, and we only hired them when they were billable."

However, many of those internal staffers were unhappy and thinking about leaving. Whenever anyone made a mistake or did not meet a goal, Jim's attitude was demeaning. "My dealings with clients and external employees were quite a bit different from the way I handled the internal employees," he recalls now. "The externals were a commodity that I had to have to deliver services. I would do anything to keep them happy. I also could use whatever social graces it took to sell a million-dollar contract, but I dealt with the people under my authority the way I would a truck that had quit running. If I couldn't tune it up, I'd just put it in the back lot and get a new one."

This was not the kind of culture the firm's owners wanted to promote. When Jim first began his executive development program, it was clear that he was doing it just to appease his boss. He had exceptional business savvy but still firmly believed that his method of handling employees was the most effective way, and, after all, he certainly had the financial results. "I didn't realize that people valued relationships and the soft side of management as they did. I was after the results: sales, profits. I felt that the people on my staff were valuable, but at the same time expendable. I put most of my skills into the relationships where people had a choice. I felt that the folks working for me were fortunate to be there. I was compensating them well, and I expected them to perform with a minimum of social grace from me."

"I come from a dysfunctional family, from poverty," Jim explains. "I had no role models in my early years. I had to fight and scratch for basic survival. So it created a tough, no-nonsense, low-compassion, no-interpersonal-skills person. I didn't realize all this; all I knew was that whatever it took to win results I could do. I never had anyone to enlighten me about nurturing your image in the eyes of other people, seeing yourself as other people see you, to cultivate loyalty and strong relationships."

Jim's fierce determination to succeed in the business world helped him change his style as a leader. "If somebody gives me criticism I try to learn from it," he says; "realizing the problem is about 90 percent of the solution, deciding this is real and that behavior needs to change. Now I realize this was one of the main things that had held me back in corporate life."

———

Bob asked Jim if he would experiment for one week. "I said, 'If it doesn't work, go right back to the way you've been.' I had him begin with just one of his direct reports: go to that person, sit down, and ask what he thought about the business and what could be improved. Jim was to figure out some way to implement the idea or use the information to help the organization prosper. He then would go back to the person and talk about how the suggestion had helped the company. Also during this week, Jim was to find multiple ways to positively reinforce and compliment his direct reports and not make one critical or negative comment. Even if something happened, Jim was to let it go, or find some other way, or let someone else deal with it. The next time we saw Jim, about two weeks later, he had already done this exercise with three of his direct reports and was planning to do the same thing with the others. He said, 'They'll do anything for me now. I can't believe the difference this is making.'"

"I began to pay close attention to every relationship," Jim says, "and to go home every day thinking, 'Is there anybody who will say something negative about what I've done?'" Asking yourself that kind of question after any conversation is an excellent strategy for improving the respectfulness of your relationships; no matter what the conflict or issue, meeting this requirement successfully forces you to solve problems without using blame. "I improved my relationships with everybody in my circle of influence," Jim says. "My wife would say I overcame things that had harmed our relationship. I learned my flaws. Key to the measure of success I had working with the program is that I wanted desperately to succeed. If I hadn't been committed to the process, we would have had only average results, not worthy of mention."

• • •

Blame is a poisonous response to problem situations. When you introduce it into relationships, it prevents others from learning and growing, and it prevents you from taking responsibility for yourself and doing the same. Moving beyond it is the key to becoming a mature person, and to releasing the full power of every other quality of Leadership Character.

Key Concepts

- Blame subverts both respect and responsibility; it promotes defensiveness rather than learning and undermines a culture of personal responsibility.

- Coercive and pacesetting styles of leadership are the least effective because they are rooted in blame.

- Moving beyond blame helps foster conflict that is creative rather than resentful and is a hallmark of successful leadership.

CHAPTER

6

Humility

Warnings about the dangers of arrogance have been around for a long time, at least since the Old Testament was written; Proverbs 16:18 reminds us, "Pride goeth before a fall, and a haughty spirit before destruction." Our experience, coaching thousands of people on the issues of Leadership Character, and numerous studies by others make it clear that insensitivity is the most frequent cause of a career being derailed and of a leader's rising star fizzling out.[1] In a 2002 paper, Fleming and Holland report:

> Quite often bright, ambitious, and confident managers fail because of personality defects such as arrogance, competitiveness, aloofness, or the tendency to micromanage. These flawed or 'darkside' interpersonal tendencies coexist with well-developed social skills, which also explains why some people with these maladaptive qualities sometimes ascend to leadership roles.[2]

It may seem paradoxical, but by breeding arrogance, success can carry within it the seed of self-destruction. Consider the fact that most accidents involving firefighters occur not when they are new on the job but after ten years' experience.

Significantly, those executives who score high on arrogance in individual personality testing are the ones least likely to be able to see themselves clearly. Compared to what their colleagues say about them in 360-degree evaluations, they overrate themselves much more often than do less arrogant leaders. About 80 percent of the executives referred to us for leadership coaching are senior-level or high-potential managers, who use our executive development program for high-level growth. The others are turnarounds, people who are recognized as valuable, but who have significant flaws that their organizations are saying will be career stoppers unless they change. These turnaround referrals also consistently test out as more arrogant than the development referrals.

Here's a common pattern: Someone is promoted or brought in from outside because she is bright, talented, hardworking, and ambitious. Those are all fine traits, and typical components of success in the world of work. We coach many of these transplanted executives, in what we call an executive integration program. Their companies want these new leaders to bring in fresh ideas; they are often hired precisely to bring in new ways of thinking. The challenge for the newcomer is to introduce these innovations in a way that works. But data show that in some organizations, close to 80 percent of executives brought in from outside fail for two primary reasons:

- The organization isn't flexible and open enough to accept them; it's like a body rejecting a transplanted organ.

- The problem is within the new executive herself. She is unappreciative of the culture she's coming into. She keeps offering ideas from her previous organization, implying that it was a better place or that the people there were more capable.

The problem is compounded if she doesn't have a personality that allows others to question her easily. Lack of humility, lack of interest in what others think, and even abrasiveness may be accepted more easily from someone in a lower position, whose specific skills are seen as valuable. Our hypothetical leader is expected to play a larger, more creative role in the overall functioning of the group, or perhaps to introduce unfamiliar ideas. Stressed by these responsibilities, she becomes more impatient, less willing to share decision making, and, ultimately, less able to influence and lead. If the particular organizational culture does not encourage honest feedback and openness, as many do not, the situation is only made worse. After all that effort to achieve a high position, because she has come to be perceived as arrogant, hostile, and offensive, she is fired.

HEADED FOR A FALL

David seemed headed for something like that. A line manager in a service subsidiary of a Fortune 100 company, he believed he had the ability to run the division but felt stuck two promotions away from that position. David is bright. He has a good academic background and many of the talents required for success in business.

"At the time we started the executive development program," he recalls, "we had an organization that was demoralized. There was a lack of motivation among many of the players, and we didn't have very good teamwork. We had some incumbents close to the top who had been there a number of years and took the attitude that 'knowledge is power' and didn't want to share it. Some of them were not formally educated and were intimidated by people who did have that kind of foundation. For example, the person who was being groomed to take over the division had limited formal education and clearly seemed the wrong choice. I was very frustrated. I felt I had the credentials and capability to offer leadership, but that there weren't any opportunities. I'd actually been told that I was too educated to be in that organization." David's frustrations with the external situation only exacerbated his tendency to be impulsive and to say what he thought without thinking it through. He had very strong ideas on many subjects, which he did not hesitate to voice—and so came to be viewed by others as argumentative, opinionated, and self-righteous.

"I had my own set of challenges," he admits now, looking back. "I had come out of the U.S. Air Force and often felt that the way we did it there was right, and I verbalized that a little too much." Of course, when he did this, he only saw himself as suggesting better approaches. "In many cases they were better ways, but the organization wasn't receptive to change, and I also didn't have the skill sets to make it happen. I was fortunate to have been trained in leadership and management in the service; a lot of people in today's business environment don't get that kind of experience and training early on. One thing you don't learn there, though, is how to manage change from the middle; the military is a top-down structure."

Even though by this time David had been with the company for several years, he says, "I made a lot of the classic mistakes people make when they come in from outside, in not respecting the organization. I wasn't doing myself any favors." He wasn't able to offer his ideas in a way that worked. When we began to work with him, both David's personality assessment data and his 360-degree review feedback showed him to have problems with arrogance, being too opinionated, and not being enough of a team player. We'll look at his full story after a discussion of humility and ways people display—or fail to display—it. Leading is not about telling people what to do.

When given a new position of responsibility, whether they've just been elected chair of a Rotary committee, promoted to first-level supervision, or made a vice president, many people begin automatically to think of the orders they will issue, the decisions they will make, how they will sweep out the cobwebs and do things differently. They start making lists of tasks for others to do. They seem to assume that because they now have this formal role, they've suddenly been endowed with all the necessary skills and knowledge to manage the group. We can certainly understand this impulse. Faced with big new responsibilities and expectations, we all naturally feel pressure to come up with the strategy and tactics that can meet them. There's nothing wrong with that impulse per se.

However, there are several limitations in relying solely on this approach: It fails to make use of the knowledge others have to offer, and it keeps you from getting the true lay of the land, from

———

building strong relationships with your colleagues, and, perhaps most important, from ever creating an environment where your ideas are heard. The people who report to you or work with you will not be particularly motivated to support your efforts. People who feel reduced to carrying out other people's chores don't strive to make their best contributions as they do the work. If that's all you expect (and allow) from them, you may well be the nominal leader, but you won't have many willing or productive followers. It takes humility to get others to follow in ways that draw out the best they have to give, that get your own ideas heard, and that allow you to be the leader you want to be.

Lacking humility and behaving arrogantly have negative consequences, both in interpersonal relationships and in business results. Arrogant people are controlling. Things must go their way, and arrogant people lose emotional control if things don't. They act as if no one else can do anything as well as they can. They are poor at listening to input from others and thus typically don't get the feedback they need for making good decisions because people are not comfortable talking with them. Afraid perhaps of the contradictions within themselves, they don't make themselves vulnerable.

Allowing yourself to be vulnerable—sharing yourself including your imperfections—is one of the most powerful skills for success in an organization, and probably the one least effectively used. Victor Rozek writes:

> *Vulnerability invites differences of opinion, rather than fearing them. It allows the honest expression of anger, as opposed to acting out of anger. It means talking directly to a person, rather than behind his back. It acknowledges the contradictions that abound in the workplace.*[3]

Showing humility and vulnerability is like a magnet that draws other people to you and makes them open up in return. People are more willing then to be honest and forthcoming about how they see a project or venture, especially about misgivings or flaws they sense that you may not be in a position to see. Whenever company surveys are done to assess the way people view the process within an organization, almost without exception lack of open communication is the number one problem that shows up.

It is often assumed that a person who behaves in an arrogant manner is masking feelings of inferiority. Though this certainly can be the case, it is by no means always true. Some of us are just born with very strong personalities that dispose us to be more egocentric, to not focus well on others. Still, as a general rule, the more comfortable you are with your self-image, and the more self-confident, the less likely it is that you will need to act—to pretend to be—better than others.

Being humble means acknowledging your own imperfections, vulnerabilities, and limitations. It also means finding and acknowledging the value in others. Humble people don't think less of themselves; they just think more of other people. A key to developing humility is getting interested in other people. Allowing yourself to be interested in people means learning how to listen.

A LEADER'S CHALLENGE WITH EXPRESSING HUMILITY

David's Story

"The military," says David, "doesn't breed good losers, and you're darn glad it doesn't. But that might have set me up a little bit. You're trained to portray confidence in your skill set and your ability to win no matter what. That's a good attitude to have in business, too, but it's not always a good way to deal with people. You're *not* perfect in everything, and your way isn't always the right way; oftentimes there are many other ways to achieve something."

Because David had natural leadership capacity and was highly motivated to advance within his company, he was receptive to looking at the issues that were getting in his way, and to doing something about them. Fortunately, a new leader took over the division; it was he who brought us in to help. This new leader was an exceptionally well-rounded person, who was especially good at acting with humility. David was able to use him as a role model, witnessing daily the ways he handled relationships with other people.

"He is one of the most powerful leaders I've ever been around," David says. "He looks at the world positively every day, no matter what the situation. He's not a workaholic, but he has tremendous stamina. When you walk into his office, he stops everything, gets up, and comes around from behind his desk. He values everybody, and is a terrific communicator. I only heard him get the least bit stern twice in three years of working together."

As he describes this boss, you can almost hear David ticking off the elements of the Leadership Character Model: courage, self-confidence, empathy, emotional mastery, and so on. We encouraged David to pay attention to this leader's good example, but we also asked him to directly confront the arrogant attitude he had formed about his co-workers.

"Bob suggested that I take a pad and write down something positive about every individual in the organization, even those I didn't care much for," David explains. "It's easier than you might think. Then in some way I was to work the positive thing into conversation with each person and help that individual feel good about himself. That was a pretty tall order for me, but the reaction was very positive, and when you get positive reactions from people, that builds your own self-esteem. It starts you toward reframing the way you feel about other people, though that does take time. But you're now actually connecting. You get a sense of how to value other individuals, and how to communicate that to them."

"Before, I had told a lot of people about better ways to do things, and I'd been pretty vocal about the need for people to enhance their education. I needed to develop my active listening, where instead I had been doing a lot of active telling. I wasn't building relationships in which people *gave me permission* to give them suggestions."

David adds, "That great leader I was fortunate to work for? He moved on, to go fix some other department. I have his job now."

When we first worked with David's department, we conducted an organizational effectiveness profile, measuring it against some

500 other big corporate departments. It scored well below the norm in almost every category. "Now," says David, "the organization has gone from two standard deviations below the norm on most of those criteria to two standard deviations above the norm on all but about four. We've been able to sustain that and grow our performance. I credit my predecessor with setting the foundation blocks in place. He allowed leaders to emerge within the organization."

• • •

HUMBLE LEADERSHIP

Leaders who are humble tend to be more concerned with getting results than with thanks or recognition. Their openness to other people's ideas and their generosity with praise, making the people they are around feel valued and respected, can liberate enormous amounts of energy, yielding real riches.

Jim Collins, author of *Good to Great,* studied how some companies manage to shift from only average performance to really outstanding performance, and what factors allow them to sustain that excellence. His research shows that the very best leaders, who guide just such shifts, have a combination of two qualities that separate them from even very good leaders. Collins names these *fierce resolve* and *genuine humility.* These leaders were not heroic, larger-than-life, charismatic figures—not the flamboyant, egocentric celebrity execs you recognize from their talk-show appearances and best-selling books, like Lee Iacocca or Jack Welch. In a down-to-earth sense humble leaders may be true heroes, but few people outside their own circles ever know their names.

This idea that the most effective leaders are deeply humble, and Collins's corollary observation that they are often quiet, retiring, and subdued in their manner, contradicts popular expectation, and much previous management theory as well. Yet it was Collins's inescapable conclusion, based on data he collected from nearly 1,500 companies that had appeared on the Fortune 500 list. These top leaders embody both humility and resolve, respect and responsibility, the soft and hard aspects of character; they are people who could embrace this polarity and draw power from it. They not only turned their companies around, achieving the transition from mediocrity to excellence, but also left those organizations with a legacy of enduring resilience and success. "Throughout our interviews with such executives," Collins writes, "we were struck by the way they talked about themselves—or rather, didn't talk about themselves. They'd go on and on about the company and the contribution of other executives, but they would instinctively deflect discussion about their own role."

Accepting the truth that humility underlies the most powerful leadership demands that we make some clear distinctions. Modesty does not equal weakness. To be shy is not to be fearful. Outward placidity can hide inner intensity and stoic resolve. Respect for other people, which is intangible, has results on the bottom line that you can really count.

It was the need to illustrate the power of respect and the importance of balance to just the kind of leaders who view themselves as no-nonsense, tough, and results focused that inspired the Leadership Character Model. It is an especially effective tool for change with these leaders, who are frequently arrogant and claim to have little time for what they view as the soft skills of relating to people. The simple pictorial representation of the scale helps them see that being respectful need not take away from their ability to get results, but that, instead, cultivating the qualities of respect, such as humility, gives their leadership balance.

Another idea that helps drive this point home is Servant Leadership. Articulated by Robert Greenleaf, this concept turns the organizational pyramid upside down.[4] The leader, it asserts, perhaps counterintuitively, is present to serve the front line and the rest of the organization, not the other way around. It is up to the leader to do whatever it takes to draw out the best participation of everyone else. Many great executives buy the Servant Leadership idea because it yields results. Herb Kelleher, the CEO of Southwest Airlines, applies it quite literally. Years ago we were discussing

Southwest Airlines with a management team; one member of the group had just been on a Southwest flight. He said that Herb Kelleher was on the flight, and he was amazed when Kelleher donned an apron and served in the cabin along with the flight attendants. We have since learned that that is typical behavior for Kelleher. In an era when most airlines can barely escape bankruptcy, Southwest has been an industry phenomenon. Surely the attitude of humility represented by the company's top leader is one key to the company's success.

ONE LEADER'S EMBRACE OF HUMILITY RIPPLES THROUGH AN ORGANIZATION

Tony's Story

Tony was the president and CEO of a public relations and advertising firm. At a time when his organization was growing very fast, he made a commitment to developing his entire executive team's leadership skills and culture.

In his own 360-degree review, Tony was viewed as too controlling. He was not very open to the ideas of other people, who said he often slowed things down by insisting on approving every detail in advance, no matter how minor it might be. He constantly second-guessed others and often countermanded their decisions. He would not disclose any of the company's financial information except to one or two other people.

PERCEPTION VS. SELF-PERCEPTION

When Tony saw this feedback, he was shaken. "I argued with it," he recalls. "I looked at myself as an involved, engaging, interactive, communicating, part-of-the-team kind of guy. The fact that I was perceived as controlling was a slap-in-the-head surprise to me— that people felt it was so very difficult to sway my opinion. It was hard to accept that an outside perception was different from a self-perception, and that it was so frustrating for other people. When I would discount somebody's perspective as not being the right solution, they felt they weren't being given fair consideration. I just viewed it as that I appreciated a good argument."

Tony's image of himself was not one of someone who was arrogant. Rather, he saw himself as a kind, caring father. This *benevolent parent* style of leadership is quite common in our business culture. Though Tony may have been viewed as somewhat more autocratic and domineering than would typically be expected from the benevolent parent style, the fact was he vacillated between arrogance and benevolence. The difficulty is that neither of these styles of leadership creates a sense of equity with others. In the company survey that was done, sure enough, overall communication was generally viewed as being very poor. It was unsettling to the people who worked for Tony that they did not feel knowledgeable about the financial status of the company or its general direction or even have much clarity regarding what was going on outside their particular area.

As it was for Tony, arrogance is a blind spot that is very difficult to see and very challenging to overcome. True humility is something that develops over a lifetime, a correlate of wisdom that naturally develops as people age and come to see the limits of their own experience, personality, and worldview. But once he was aware that other people perceived him this way, Tony was able to realize the value of creating a greater sense of equity within the company. Still, when he decided to change, he found that because his habits had been well practiced and were part of his repertoire, it was not easy for him.

SEEING IT FROM THEIR SIDE

Tony had to push himself to discuss issues from others' points of view, to listen and reflect and then give them feedback about how he used their input to help the organization. He set up meetings with his people, individually and as a team, for just this purpose. Opening up information about the company's financial picture was the last in a series of things he brought himself to do to move toward more of a partnership-style leadership. As he did so, though, he was visibly happier because he was sharing some of the stresses and burdens rather than feeling he had to solve all the problems and do everything himself. All of this helped to create a greater sense of ownership by everybody in the organization. Because of the changes Tony made, people felt more valued and more trusted by him and this, in turn, made them want to help the company thrive.

"I learned a greater appreciation for listening to where people were coming from, and for allowing discussion. Our staff meetings became more regular, more of a forum. We worked out a more formal structure in which a leadership team spends time together. I realize that I am fairly strong-willed. But also, where it used to be easy to see myself as one of the guys, I recognize that with the title I've got, and the real control I've got, it's hard for other people to think of me as just another vote around the table. I didn't realize how difficult that made it—how threatening—for other people to be more forceful. I also saw that the strength of each individual's talents and personality needed to be brought out and plugged in more. Like, here's a creative person who brings an introverted approach to solving problems; the importance there is just to shut up and listen. Leaders do need to exercise some control but do so by creating inclusion and the opportunity to be significantly involved. That's the struggle for me. What needs to go with that is a willingness from other people to jump into that participatory role."

When the first executive group in Tony's firm started the development program, he remembers, "The initial group feeling was, 'This is a bunch of HR stuff and we're not that cranked about doing it.' We wondered, 'Is this just wasting a bunch of money and time?' Like all these kinds of things, it's hard to equate this to a specific bottom-line result, but in the process, it was fun to watch how often and how willingly people would share." Tony said, "They would come back from a Leadership Character training meeting and say, 'Guess how people perceive me! I've got this trait I've got to work on,' and other people would say, 'Duh, of course you do.' We all found out things about ourselves that were interesting. I know I'm less controlling now, though I'm sure I would still be perceived in a 360 as a close-to-the-vest guy. But I'm aware of it more. Awareness is a powerful tool."

• • •

Perhaps more than any other single quality, humility is emblematic of the kind of leadership our organizations so critically need today. The old command model, suffused with arrogance and rigidity, no longer works. When it's steeped in humility, leadership becomes expansive, resilient, and in touch.

Key Concepts

- Arrogance is an obstacle to clear perception, and a major cause of leadership failure.

- Humility isn't thinking less of yourself; it's thinking more of others.

- Humble leaders are more concerned with results than personal recognition.

- Humble leaders find value in others, and others are inspired to follow them.

PART THREE

RESPONSIBILITY— THE POWER TO ACT

7

Accountability

In chapter 2 we mentioned the work of Robert Kaplan and Robert Kaiser, in which they use the terms *forceful* and *enabling* to mean essentially what we mean when we describe the leadership qualities of responsibility and respect. Kaplan and Kaiser write:

> *When a leader develops and balances strengths on both sides, it pairs two good things that are seeming opposites. It puts them in tension with each other and in so doing brings out the dynamic relationship between them. Objectively, forceful leadership and enabling leadership are complements of each other. But many managers don't see it that way. They see one side as being preferable to the other.*[1]

Moreover, when Kaplan analyzed his research and consulting experience with senior managers,

> *It wasn't just lopsidedness that stood out. It was the connection to effectiveness. When the data on a manager indicated that he or she was out of balance, more often*

---

than not that was a manager who received a relatively low rating on overall effectiveness. And by the same token, managers who coworkers described as "balanced" or "complete" tended to get relatively high effectiveness ratings. This effect seemed to make a big difference.[2]

In Part 2, we examined the essential elements of respect: empathy, emotional mastery, lack of blame, and humility. These are all qualities most typically thought of as people oriented and soft, rather than results oriented and resolute, as if having soft qualities might make a person nice, but not necessarily strong. Now it's true that to lead with decency you must be sensitive and vulnerable; those qualities are strengths. Successful, authentic leadership is also bold and confident, far-seeing and persistent. No one is against being nice per se (although, as you'll see later in this chapter, an excessive need to be nice can get a leader into trouble). The reason respect, in all its essential aspects, is crucial to good leadership is that it creates a synergy with the other side of the scale, making possible the most powerful expression of the core qualities of responsibility: accountability, courage, self-confidence, and focus on the whole.

RESPONSIBILITY IN ACTION

In the next four chapters, we will examine those four key elements of responsibility. First, though, let's look at one of the best models of responsibility in action to be found in recent American business history. The story of IBM's turnaround illustrates the power that results when individuals, regardless of the positions they happen to occupy in a hierarchy, act with courage and self-confidence, keep the big picture in mind, and demand accountability from both themselves and their organizations.

Although it had pioneered personal computing, by the early '90s IBM had lost touch with the directions of both the marketplace and the technology, and lost two-thirds of its market capitalization, too. Specifically, the company was ignoring a small but rapidly burgeoning phenomenon called the World Wide Web.

David Grossman had joined the company a few years earlier as a midlevel programmer, and he happened to be an early Internet geek. He could imagine both the possibilities of the Web and the risks of ignoring it. In 1992, IBM was the official technology sponsor of the Winter Olympics, collecting and displaying competition results during the games. Grossman realized that these data were being used by another computer company to provide content on its own Web site. He alerted IBM's head of marketing that their data feed was being ripped off. Then he went further, arranging to give a demonstration of the Web to some senior marketing executives.

Grasping the transformative potential of the Internet was a challenge for many of us a decade or so ago, and not everyone Grossman spoke to in the company got it right away, either. One who did was John Patrick, a career IBM employee who was on a strategy task force and kept an eye out for the next big thing. "Patrick and Grossman became IBM's Internet tag team," wrote Gary Hamel, a Harvard Business School research fellow, "with Patrick doing the business translation for Grossman, and Grossman doing the technology translation for Patrick."[3] (Hamel's full account of this story is available as a reprint from the *Harvard Business Review*. It makes a great, quick lesson in accountability.)

The two devised a strategy to find and enlist the many other nascent Net-heads in the organization, to bring senior-level attention to establishing a corporate presence on the Web and to spreading the culture of the Internet within the organization. This meant confronting skepticism, parochialism, and reluctance to change. Hamel describes them as "throwing Internet hand grenades," but they were doing that with a broad vision of where the company should be going and a confidence that they could affect its direction and success, and they did. IBM is now a major player in the world of e-business technology.

"Again and again, throughout their Internet campaign, Patrick and Grossman broke long-standing IBM rules and overstepped the boundaries of their own authority," Hamel observes, "but because their cause was so important and their commitment to IBM's success so visibly selfless, they got away with things that had often sunk careers at Big Blue. Then and now, Patrick is unapologetic. 'If you think of yourself as being in a box with boundaries, you're not going to have any breakthroughs.'"[4]

ACCOUNTABILITY MEANS OWNING THE WHOLE THING

People often complain that they have been given "responsibility without authority." There's a real problem in being asked to do something when you lack the authority to make the decisions and requests the task requires, but too often people use this as an excuse for passivity or for failing to build their own ability to influence things. Forget authority: few people really have it anymore anyway. Build your influence skills instead, and get on with the job.

We're fortunate to have an inspiring model of accountability in our own office. Susan Hitchcock was our first professional hire. For twenty-four years before that, she had been a manager in the Network organization, that part of BellSouth that's really a telephone company. Bob says, "Her previous boss told us, 'Susan hasn't ever done the job that you're asking her to do, but if she says that she can do it, grab her, because she will!'"

"Susan is one of the few people I've ever met whose respect and relationship skills match her penchant for accountability," Lyn says. "She's in early every morning, even though she has no set hours. She once told me that she felt she wasn't as sharp as she used to be. Then she added, in complete seriousness, that she thought it might be because she now got up at 5:00 a.m. instead of at 4:00 a.m."

In a small company like ours, there really are no job descriptions, but Susan wouldn't pay attention even if there were. If there's a client coming in early, Susan checks the schedule to be sure she's in the office to greet our visitor, even though that's clearly not her job. If there's a mailing to go out, she stuffs and stamps envelopes, although we have administrative staff to do that. She recently went to set up a conference room at 6:00 p.m. for a workshop the next morning, even though she wasn't leading the workshop. She just *does* things, without even asking whose responsibility they're supposed to be.

With us, her early responsibilities were primarily client relations, marketing, and business development, but she has a passion for issues faced by women in leadership. She developed and now directs our Women in Leadership Initiative. She carries this spirit into the community, too. She was one of the founding board members of the Board of Directors Network, which is devoted to placing more women on corporate boards. Susan has served on the boards of other organizations concerned with women's leadership, and with literacy. She works hard at being a good role model within our business and within the community at large.

CHANGE YOUR QUESTION

The working title for this book was *Going First: Quit Waiting for Leadership.* That says it all about accountability. Accountability means you, individually, taking ownership for the success of any enterprise you are involved in. It means seeing yourself, regardless of your specific role or position, as providing creativity, innovation, and leadership, as well as the elbow grease required to get things done. That was certainly the attitude Patrick and Grossman took at IBM. Rather than sitting around futilely wondering, "Why doesn't management see the importance of the Internet?" they changed the question, and asked themselves, "What can we do to raise awareness of this new technology and its implications for this company?" It's the same attitude we saw at BellSouth's Fleming Island facility, described in chapter 3, where the dispiriting statement "But it's not my job" is very rarely heard. Accountability means changing the question in your life from "Why don't they . . . ?" to "What can I . . . ?"

———

Lyn's mother was one of the first women to earn an MBA at the University of Georgia and later served as assistant director of its Bureau of Business Research. She was a powerful role model in many things, including an attitude of accountability. Lyn remembers, "She didn't tolerate it when after something had gone wrong at the bureau, such as an error in a publication, people grumbled, 'Well, I *thought* that wasn't right,' or 'I could have *told* you so.' She always said, 'If you could have, then you should have.' Today, when someone at our office says something like that, I feel annoyed, too, but I realize that even though I need to push them to be accountable (which includes speaking up when they know something is wrong), I also need to move beyond that—to look at myself and change the question I'm asking. I need to ask myself, 'What could I do to improve things? Could I be more open and approachable, for instance? Could I be asking explicitly for more input?'"

The very best leaders are able to do this, but it doesn't come naturally to most of us. It takes continuous self-monitoring and the ability to balance the sensitivity to others that comes from developing respect with a willingness to hold yourself and others accountable for the work of the whole. If you want to be accountable, you have to quit wishing the other person or group would do something to change a situation; think instead of what you can do. If you're a midlevel manager or an individual contributor, stop saying, "The senior leaders should tell us where we're headed" or "Why isn't the company paying attention to this new trend I'm aware of?" If you're a senior leader, stop hunting for excuses to explain away sales results you aren't happy with and start asking what you can do to improve them next time. The mind-set of accountability is an attitude of taking full responsibility, and this applies not only at work but in every aspect of life.

If you are married, with a mind-set of accountability you see yourself as taking 100 percent responsibility for the success of the relationship. With any luck, your spouse wants to take 100 percent responsibility for its success, too. However, you don't control your spouse's behavior (or your boss's, or your direct reports', or anybody else's); you can only control your own. Often, people will say,

———

"I'll meet her halfway." But if you hold on to the idea of taking 100 percent responsibility for the situation or relationship, you always have somewhere to go and something to do, a way to be an instrument for improvement. This does not mean you do everything to make the relationship successful and your spouse is expected to do nothing. That would also be irresponsible on both your parts, and an obviously unhealthy, even doomed, dynamic for a marriage. With a mind-set of accountability, you know you are always capable of brainstorming possible solutions to any problem by yourself *or* with whoever else is involved. Without this attitude, it's easy to abdicate responsibility altogether and then blame the other person when things don't work out.

REPLACE COMPLAINT WITH COMMITMENT

Here is an exercise you can use to change the question in your life from "Why don't they . . . ?" to "What can I . . . ?" (It is a simplified version of one presented in *How the Way We Talk Can Change the Way We Work* by Robert Kegan and Lisa Lahey, a book we strongly recommend to anyone who wants to develop personal accountability.)[5]

Draw four columns on a piece of paper. At the top of the page, write a complaint you have at work or at home, such as, "People at work are always gossiping about other people." Now, in the first column, write out what you're committed to: the value or deeply held belief that is reflected in the complaint. In this example, you might write, "I am committed to directness and forthrightness, to talking to people, not about them."

Next, ask yourself if there is anything at all that you do that keeps the unsatisfactory situation going, even though you don't like it. Write that in the second column. In this example, many people will recognize at this point that they often listen when others gossip, which actually encourages more gossip.

In the third column, write your answer to the question, "What competing commitment do I have that prevents me from honoring my original commitment?" Despite that lofty idea of yourself as somebody who doesn't tolerate gossip, for example, you might find that you have another commitment (or need) that is getting in your way. Maybe it's that you want to be part of the crowd and to feel liked. Just verbalizing your conflicting commitments in this way will get you started on purposely choosing the behaviors you really want to exhibit and eliminating the ones that do not serve you well.

In the fourth column, write the big assumption that keeps the behavior going and keeps you from acting on the commitment you listed in the first column. In the case of tolerating gossip, your big underlying assumption might be that if you aren't liked and if you aren't part of the crowd, you'll be isolated, alone, and weakened.

Kegan and Lahey say that the silent chatter in our minds usually leaves us torn between, on one hand, "becoming preoccupied with our complaints and creating elaborate narratives about their origins, costs, and consequences—rich dramas in which we usually cast ourselves at the center as well-intentioned, beleaguered victim-heroes," and on the other hand, "telling ourselves to stay positive, and not get bogged down in all this unproductive negativity."[6] They point out that neither alternative is helpful. The value of this four-column exercise is that it asks you to articulate the ideas you hold that can drive your behavior even when you aren't conscious of them. By examining the competing commitments and underlying, unconscious assumptions that keep you from changing, you can begin to live from a strong, centered, responsible place, embracing the power you have to shape your own experience.

STRETCH YOUR DEFINITION OF ACCOUNTABILITY

People have an almost uncanny ability to deny and rationalize, and in particular to deflect and avoid accountability. Maybe the problem lies in how people define this idea. Being accountable is typically thought of in a very limited way, only as being answerable—in other words, liable, or potentially held at fault. A negative, and even frightening, feeling attaches to that idea. After all, who likes being blamed when things go wrong?

Being answerable for what you do certainly is one aspect of accountability. We call that *personal accountability*, and it is fundamental to acting with integrity in any organization or social situation. People who are personally accountable get things done when they say they will; manage their time well, especially when they know somebody else is paying them for it; follow through on commitments and promises; and are responsive, returning phone calls promptly, for just one small example. Personal accountability is what people need when they first enter the workforce, and it's often what first gets them recognized and promoted to leadership positions or asked to play informal leadership roles.

Another aspect of accountability takes you beyond that self-responsibility, when you enlarge your view and accept responsibility for the success of the collective effort. People who can do that think and behave like owners, even when they're not. We expect this perspective from managers and executives, although many of them don't consistently deliver it. The IBM story shows how powerful it can be coming from those far from the top of the hierarchy. Remember, a similarly large-minded aspect of accountability is taking 100 percent responsibility for relationships, rather than meeting people halfway.

Holding others accountable is also essential, especially for anyone in a formal position of leadership. For that, mutual planning and setting explicit goals are required, as is having clearly agreed-upon measures for success. Otherwise, people can't know what's expected of them. Following up and following through with those to whom you delegate become key. One of the most frequent complaints we hear from people in almost every company we work with is the lack of that kind of engagement and involvement on the part of bosses. People, especially the most productive, committed people, also complain mightily when managers allow others on the team to coast and not pull their weight. Being engaged, involved, and willing to hold others accountable is an important part of responsible leadership, whether you're managing a department,

———

chairing a fund-raising drive, or leading a project team. It often means being willing to confront others and deal with conflict.

The need to be "requiring" of others, and the conflict it can generate, often gives people the negative feeling that demanding accountability will destroy relationships with those they supervise. That was an issue for Karen, who tells her story next. She went through our executive development program to become a leader who, in everyday practice, has a profound understanding of the give-and-take of real accountability. We mentioned to her that we wanted to use her story here, to illustrate how she improved in accountability. She was taken aback for a moment; it seemed to her we were implying that she used to be someone who didn't honor her word or follow through on commitments.

On the contrary, Karen, who managed a technical department, saw herself as very accountable, at least personally. She followed through on every promise. She probably recognized at some level that she should hold others accountable, too. She had definitely been told in performance appraisals that she wasn't tough enough, didn't adequately hold her direct reports to their commitments, didn't ask enough of others, and did too much of the work herself to take up the slack. After working on these issues, Karen became a model of someone who learned that accountability is not only about your own actions, but also about what you bring out in others, and that when you hold others accountable, relationships actually become more creative, productive, and responsible.

THE TROUBLE WITH NICE

Karen's Story

Karen was referred to us because she was thought of as having potential to move to higher levels of responsibility in the future. The person she reported to viewed her as having tremendous assets in building relationships with people. She was also seen as

——

an extremely hard worker, willing to do whatever it took to get the job done, and as having a very high standard of integrity. In most situations, she was able to see the big picture, and how her own organization's accomplishments helped fulfill the larger corporation's mission. Her boss was concerned, however, that Karen's results were not as good as they could be because she was so concerned with being nice that it was difficult for her to hold other people accountable.

Karen's boss's concerns were validated by both personality test data and her 360-degree feedback. We could tell that Karen was certainly assertive and confident in working with self-starters, those highly motivated achievers who need very little supervision. However, she had a large number of direct reports who needed more direction, feedback, and coaching from her than she was comfortable giving. Karen had always achieved stellar results from her individual contributions, but now she was in a position where her success depended on how well she was able to help others to be successful. Yet she was very uncomfortable telling others what to do. When she tried, she felt as if she were imposing and backed off. When there were problems, or some type of discipline was needed, she would completely avoid the situation. People began to think she had different standards for different people. There was also some resentment developing among the high-achieving direct reports toward the others, whom they viewed as not pulling their weight.

SOLVING THE CONFLICT AVOIDANCE PROBLEM

"In working through the Leadership Character Model," Karen says, "I learned how to overcome conflict avoidance, which had been hard for me. It's important to be liked, but not to the extent that you can't make the hard decisions because you're worried that people are not going to like you anymore."

One tool used in the program, the Problem-Solving Worksheet (Exercise 1, on page 128), proved especially valuable to

EXERCISE 1

Problem-Solving Worksheet

Problem theme: _____

State the problem. What would you like to change, i.e., a behavior, attitude, feeling, characteristic, etc.? How or why is it a problem for you?

Give examples. Think of situations at work and in your personal life.

Describe the situational drivers or triggers for the problem. How long have you been aware of it? When, where, how often does it occur? When it occurs, what's going on? Who else is present?

Describe your self-talk. What are you thinking or saying to yourself when it occurs?

Why haven't you dealt with the problem before? What inhibits you from making changes? What reinforces your current state?

Where are you now? On a scale of 1–10 where would you rate your current status?

What is your change goal? On a scale of 1–10 where would you rate your desired change goal?

What actions should you take now to begin the change process? What should you *stop* doing? What should you *start* doing?

What are the negative consequences of not changing?

———

Karen. This questionnaire helps people articulate the obstacles they face in becoming stronger leaders and the steps they can take to start changing those behaviors. "I had a complete epiphany when I used the worksheet to figure out why I avoided conflict," Karen says. "I've told so many people about how powerful that worksheet is. As you walk through the steps you're actually asking yourself questions like 'What is reinforcing the behavior? What's going on in my head when I do it?' They're very specific, thought-provoking questions that allow you to think about yourself and to realize that you can control your behavior if you stop and think about it. Without the worksheet questions I would never have dissected the problem.

"I saw that the real root of my avoidance of conflict was that I don't like people being mad at me, but I thought, 'What's the worst that could happen?' So they yell at you! It's not like somebody's going to physically hurt you. There's isn't really anything to be afraid of. Realizing that, I saw that I could take it head-on."

LEVERAGING ALL HER SKILLS

With this realization, Karen was able to provide the coaching that was appropriate for her people's different levels of confidence and competence. She began to see how her excellent interpersonal skills could be leveraged to work with people in a way that didn't make her feel imposing but instead allowed her to feel helpful. She came to see that the positive relationships she had actually established with each of her direct reports made it possible for her to talk with them about issues regarding their work without it "breaking the relationship." She was also able to learn to not catastrophize about someone not liking her if she gave them feedback that they did not want to hear. She says, "It's about emotional mastery, too—separating yourself a bit—and of course courage. I learned that as a leader, if you don't address a problem employee, it reflects more on you than on them."

•   •   •

___

ENGAGED LEADERS

Karen learned that an accountable leader does not simply answer for her own actions but also makes the effort to stay involved with the people she leads, whether they're doing well *or* need extra support. Of course, the nature of this engagement has to be appropriate for the specific level of competence and confidence the other person has, as well as any particular problems that exist. One size does not fit all, and just putting together an all-purpose façade of interest won't get you very far. Here's where those skills of empathy, humility, emotional mastery, and lack of blame come into play and allow you to build your responsibility. They help you to truly perceive the other person and not filter what you see through issues of your own.

For leading others in a way that fosters accountability—and in a way that balances respect and responsibility—we like the Situational Leadership model, which was co-developed by Ken Blanchard, best known as the author of the *One Minute Manager* series, and Paul Hersey.[7] On the one hand, this model distinguishes between leadership styles in terms of the amount and kind of direction and support a leader gives; it posits that effective leaders are versatile enough to shift from one style to another when appropriate. On the other hand, Situational Leadership recognizes that the right style of coaching and support is not an abstract thing but depends intimately on the developmental level, confidence, and competencies of the person receiving it. An approach like this increases a manager's ability to hold others accountable by providing a method for evaluating the amount of involvement his direct reports need. It allows the manager to continually assess and calibrate what he needs to do at any given time to help the direct report be maximally successful. It also provides a useful framework for both the manager and direct report to talk comfortably about their relationship and mutual expectations.

LEARNING FROM FAILURE

Larry's Story

Clearly, a person who tends to be disconnected from other people will have a big challenge in building accountable relationships, as you'll see with Larry. His background included many years as a very high-level financial expert, but in an individual contributor role. Then he was made CEO of a private investment firm. Things did not go well, and he was asked to step down and take a lesser assignment. Larry had never suffered any kind of failure in his career to this point. He was shaken but determined to do something about the situation, and he sought help in figuring out what he could have done differently. It says a lot about him that he insisted on paying for his work in his executive development program from his own pocket (these expenses are almost always covered by a person's company). He wanted to invest in his own development, to see if he could build the skills necessary to move back into the top leadership role and stay there.

HOW THEY SAW LARRY

Larry was a puzzle. His personality data indicated he had personality characteristics typical of engaged, successful leaders. However, it was also clear that he had an independent, self-sufficient, almost loner style. Though Larry was viewed as very bright and having strong business savvy, he was seen as having been unsuccessful in building his team. People saw him as aloof and disengaged unless there was a major crisis, and then he would engage but in a critical, fault-finding manner. People in his company didn't see him as accountable. His follow-through was lacking, and he was perceived as unwilling to get down in the trenches. He was viewed as ineffective in managing direct reports, and as an assiduous avoider of conflict.

People thought he didn't have his heart in the job. Larry had enjoyed great success as a financial expert on Wall Street, but that was a role that didn't require leading and managing other people. He had been a deal superstar, not an accomplished manager. Nobody questioned his brilliance and desire for the company to succeed, but people suspected that he wasn't "hungry" enough now to be fully committed. Larry was in over his head. Yet his personality assessment data showed him to be the kind of person who should be good with follow-through and conscientious about managing others. His 360-degree feedback was full of comments about his not dealing with the performance problems of direct reports, avoiding decisions, and making promises he couldn't keep in order to circumvent conflict. One peer who contributed to his 360-degree review questioned his credibility, his over-promising, and his paying too much attention to cultivating the boss.

After a person's evaluations are gathered from people within the same company, they are compared to information on thousands of others, in a database that includes CEOs, presidents, and other senior leaders. Against that group, Larry's scores were so low, particularly in the areas that had to do with accountability and team building, that we wondered whether trying to do the job of a CEO just might have been too difficult for him, and not within his repertoire of talents. But after reading nearly fifty pages of comments, both positive and negative, from his 360-degree data, Larry said, "I know from these negative comments that the person being described would never be placed in a CEO role, but with your help and my hard work, I think I can fix all of these problems." In a comment that reflected his determination and propensity for accountability, he added, "And I want to do this—period."

LARRY'S TRANSFORMATION

Larry's first assignment was to sit down with each direct report, set goals, and then meet with each person regularly to go over progress and coach or provide support as necessary. He was to attend periodic staff meetings of his direct reports. As he became more engaged, he became more decisive and direct. He knew more about what was going on in all parts of the business and felt more confident making decisions. Larry began turning things around and changing the way he was viewed by building relationships within the context of helping each person be successful in his or her projects and goals. In meetings, he became more focused on the mission and objectives of his team, and much more engaged in providing real support in helping the team accomplish its goals. There were two particular peers with whom he had had some conflict, and a significant amount of tension had built up between them. Larry decided to take 100 percent accountability for those relationships, and within a few months he turned them both around. He talked openly to his colleagues about his behavior and the things he could see he had been doing that were not helpful or productive. For example, he knew that one of the things the peers were bothered about was that he had a direct report who wasn't doing her job and they had seen Larry not holding her accountable for her poor performance.

Looking back, Larry says, "Many of the things that made me ineffective, such as not following through, not building a cohesive, competent team, not making the right decisions, and so on, were a product of my lack of knowledge, my insecurity. I was masking that, without realizing it. I can see now why people thought that I was insincere and didn't have my heart in it." Larry worked hard at ferreting out his blind spots and doing something about them; he became much more engaged and accountable. Within two years, Larry's "transformation," as others in the firm termed it, led to the announcement that he was being renamed CEO. This move was strongly endorsed by all the senior team members.

• • •

POWER FOR ALL THE PEOPLE

Larry, obviously, was a top leader, but no matter where you are in an organization, it is your job to be accountable. Once again, that means not only being answerable but also being willing to look at issues in new and creative ways and acting as if the success of the whole enterprise depends on what you do. Regardless of what their jobs may be, we often ask clients to try viewing themselves as if they were actually the president of the company, or even the owner.

In doing this visualization, they begin to see themselves as responsible for the success of their relationships with every other person in the company and for the success of the business as a whole. This simple mental exercise makes a great difference in how the leaders go about their jobs. They say, "Before, I was very focused on my own department, and on supporting or protecting my own people. But the larger view helps me be less turf oriented, and more concerned with the success of the entire company. If everyone in the organization felt and thought this way, what a powerful organization it could be!"

Leaders must remember, as Larry learned, that in managing large numbers of people, you cannot be personally accountable without recognizing that a huge part of your job is to be engaged with people, on top of things, and disciplined enough in your monitoring of the organization that you get things done through other people. It is hitting a balance between the skills of responsibility and those of respect, so you are not only aware of what needs to be accomplished but also sensitive to the ways you can encourage your people to do it. *That* makes success possible.

___

Key Concepts

- Accountability means not just being answerable for what you do yourself but also owning the whole thing; leaders who are accountable take responsibility for the success of the collective effort.

- The key to holding others accountable is to be actively engaged with them.

- Holding others accountable sometimes requires exercising strong leadership and getting past the need to simply be nice.

8

Courage

The first thing the word *courage* usually brings to mind is a willingness to take risks. But people are not likely to use the term to describe situations where the risks are mainly physical, as in skydiving or bungee jumping. Those kinds of activities require audacity or daring (and they can also be expressions of thrill seeking or even recklessness). People understand courage, rather, to mean a willingness to take risks for a higher cause or set of values; to act rather than crumple in the face of obstacles, to be strong even when threatened. Courage is facing a threat that could kill you, such as a diagnosis of cancer, or something that could flip your life upside down, such as discovering a pattern of fraud that might mean doom for the company in which you've made your career.

LEADING WITH COURAGE

Bob has always treasured a comment made by his late brother. John, who was 15 years older, had reenlisted in the navy in 1946 to go with Admiral Byrd on his last expedition to the South Pole. John was at the helm of Byrd's ship when it was caught up in a cyclone. The heavy winds and seas nearly capsized it. Men were being tossed from one end of the deck to the other. It was bedlam—people screaming, some crying. "When John told me this story," Bob remembers, "I asked, 'Weren't you scared?' In his slow, southern drawl, John replied, 'I didn't have time to be scared. I had to take care of my men.' Whenever I need to shore up my courage, I remind myself of this story."

We use the word *courage* to describe bravery in battle, or the fortitude it takes to stand up against situations that are clearly immoral, such as the laws that once mandated racial segregation in the American South or apartheid in South Africa. Daring and audacity by themselves demand strength, but they aren't necessarily related to integrity; they usually involve an element of showing off or proving something. Selfless bravery, the willingness to take a risk just because it's the right thing to do, and because it could benefit a larger group, is courage in the truest sense.

It's intriguing to consider the word's origins. *Courage* comes to us from the Old French for *heart* and *spirit.* Some of its earlier meanings in English are obscure now, but they still can enlarge our understanding of the concept: "intention, purpose, vital energy." When you combine these ideas with that notion of selfless bravery, courage becomes a powerful concept. Reflect again on integrity as the foundation of character, at the base of the Leadership Character Model. Your integrity is enhanced when you work on any of the eight essential qualities of respect and responsibility discussed throughout this book. Perhaps none of those eight qualities is as important for building integrity as courage.

Bypassing the Easy Path

Observing people in organizations over the years, we've seen clearly just how much courage it takes to make an ethical choice when that conflicts with an easier or more lucrative one. It takes courage, for example, not to fill an order with a slightly defective product, especially when it's a defect the customer may not notice. It takes courage not to haul a slightly overweight load, or not to simply turn away and hold your nose when a cash transaction smells fishy.

It takes courage not to pay a bribe in a country where that may be a common practice, but one that's against the explicit code of your own company.

We gained a real understanding of the courage it takes to lead with integrity many years ago, when we worked with the executive team of a small telecommunications firm that was trying to change its business model. They longed to end their dependence on customers who were either scamming the public or making money through 900 numbers, selling phone sex and the like.

This team was made up of ordinary executives, not much different from others we'd worked with. It seemed that they had found themselves in this situation almost by accident, as a small company, just taking any customers who came along, in order to survive. It was clearly hard for them to be proud of what they were doing, and because of what they were doing they had difficulty keeping employees even though they were making money. It demanded courage for them to stop taking the easy way out. Dovetailing with that courage was a willingness to look ahead and focus on the whole, to see both ethical and financial implications, to lead with an eye to the future as well as the present. (We'll talk more about focusing on the whole in chapter 10.)

We helped facilitate this process by working with the leadership team over three days in a meeting called to look at where they were, think about the kind of company and culture they wanted to become, and start action planning on getting there. They made substantial moves to segment their existing customer base, to devise plans for dropping and replacing certain segments, and to bring in other revenue. This company worked hard to figure out how to make this shift. Watching them do it, we saw how complex ethical decisions can be. Moving too quickly to sever relationships with their existing customers, for instance, would have meant laying off people, which didn't seem right either. In time, these leaders demonstrated that by focusing on your character and the character of the organization you're creating, and keeping your standards high, you'll never wind up in a place you can't be proud of.

Telling the Truth

"Courage is resistance to fear, mastery of fear, not absence of fear," Mark Twain observed. Organizations don't move forward unless they are challenged to do so, whether by external factors or from within. Many companies fail because no one is courageous enough to talk openly about the problems they perceive. If you're in the ranks, speaking truth to those in positions of power may mean risking your career. If you are in power, hearing the truth or telling the truth to the organization may mean acknowledging inadequacies in your own leadership. What holds you back from acting with courage will vary depending on your personality and your situation. Maybe what keeps you from speaking up is a desire to be liked or a reluctance to upset the routine and be thought of as a troublemaker.

The truth is that the courageous act of initiating constructive change always makes you vulnerable. That accounts for the natural protective tendency, in both individuals and social systems, to be conservative and try to keep things as they are. Whether we actually voice this or not, our first reaction to any irritant that implies a need for change is often something like, "Well, that's not how we've always done it around here before." We react this way because change can be uncomfortable. Change means uncertainty; it is often achieved only through conflict. You may have the conviction that the conflict can be constructive, but making it happen still demands a big, courageous deep breath.

Even if you are certain that what you want to say is correct, there is never a guarantee that speaking up won't somehow backfire. Anxiety and potential loss are always associated with acts of courage. That's why courage and integrity are so intimately connected. To withstand the discomfort of risk, you must hold tight to your convictions and larger goals. Of course, to do that you must already be confident that you know what those convictions and values are. At its most basic, after all, integrity is knowing what you believe and behaving consistent with that knowledge. You must articulate your values before you can act on them.

Difficult though it might be to act on your convictions, anybody can do it and have a potentially enormous impact. We can't think of three better models of courage in organizations than Sherron Watkins and Cynthia Cooper, who insisted on alerting higher-ups to patterns of accounting fraud in Enron and World-Com, respectively, and Colleen Rowley, who exposed the turf jealousy in the FBI that allowed potentially crucial advance clues to the September 11 terrorist attacks to be ignored. These women risked a great deal—disapproval at the least, and potentially their very careers—but their efforts illuminated troubling, widespread systemic problems, and the nation was grateful for that. That's why *Time* named the three Persons of the Year for 2002. The citation read: "Democratic capitalism requires that people trust in the integrity of public and private institutions alike. As whistle-blowers, these three became fail-safe systems that did not fail."[1]

BALANCING COURAGE WITH COOPERATIVENESS

To understand the complex nature of real courage, the kind with a lasting impact, like that shown by Watkins, Cooper, and Rowley, we analyzed data from the personality inventories and 360-degree reviews conducted on the thousands of organizational leaders with whom we've worked. We know that real courage in the service of a higher goal requires both the willingness to take risks for what is right and a sense of justice that creates concern for others. However, the data show that few of us are born with a perfect balance of both of these qualities.

A high tolerance for taking risky action may come with a propensity to overlook the needs of others, whereas conscientiousness about the needs of others may come with too much caution about taking bold steps. The natural leader who has both a deep concern for others and an equal amount of bravery is rare. That's why we are so inspired by people who combine a powerful sense of justice and concern for others with the courage to speak up and take extraordinary risks—the Gandhis and the Martin Luther Kings of the world.

Although most of us don't come by this balance naturally, it is certainly something we can strive for as we work to develop our Leadership Character. Typically, this lack of balance shows up in three kinds of individuals.

- The person who takes risks easily but is undeveloped in terms of ethical concerns. He is not particularly reflective; his willingness to take risks may simply be a function of impulsiveness. So his bold actions, lacking vision and intention, tend not to help the organization grow.

- The person who is highly conscientious and is rated by co-workers as very principled herself, but who has trouble taking risks. She tends to leave a situation as it is, rather than try to change it, and thus may tolerate unethical behavior in others, for example, simply by not speaking up.

- The overly self-righteous person who reduces complex situations to black and white, sees the problems in everyone else and sees himself as the conscience of the group. This person, too, is not reflective and has trouble seeing the big picture. Sometimes he is effective in pointing out a problem, but usually he overlooks its nuances. People see him as overly zealous, a crusader without humility.

Again, balance is critical for effectiveness. Real courage takes more than forcefully expressing or acting on what you think is right. It takes doing it in a way that is purposeful and reasoned, and respectful of both the complexities of situations and the needs of other people.

ACCEPTING DEFEAT, FINDING SUCCESS

Mike's Story

Mike was an affable guy with a big laugh who had built a successful sales career on his ability to win over customers. He was working as a regional sales manager in a large public company that was restructuring. He'd worked very hard over the previous year as a vice president in the marketing organization and was hoping for a promotion to a job with increased responsibility. He was in the middle of our executive development program process when one afternoon he walked into our office looking dejected and discouraged.

"He explained that he had been reassigned to a job as a sales manager," Bob recalls. "'It's a demotion,' he said, 'and I'm pretty upset about it.' Worse, the sales organization he was reassigned to had the lowest numbers in the company. Mike told me he felt betrayed and mistreated. 'There is no way that other guy should have been promoted instead of me,' he said. 'In my last job, I was number one in the sales division. All that seems forgotten now. I've given my life to this company, and this is the thanks I get! I'm going to go somewhere where I'm appreciated.'"

Bob said, "Mike, you've got at least two options here. You can feel sorry for yourself, wallow in self-pity, and make decisions based on that, or you can take the high road and use what you've already learned in this program to be an exceptional leader in your new assignment. You know it won't be hard for you to do because you've already been there, and you know the job. You could really be a great success by being passionate about it and putting your heart into it." Even as Bob said this, he could see that he had hit a nerve.

Within a few weeks, we heard from his former boss that Mike had not only accepted the position he considered a demotion but helped train his replacement in a way that he had seen no one do before, offering this person all the help he could to make sure he got off to a good start. The sales organization Mike now headed, which had been one of the weakest in the company, was also showing early and continued improvements. "I wasn't just going to lie down," Mike explains now. "I had had fun running sales teams in the past, and been successful at it. So going back to that, even though it involved swallowing my pride, still felt good. I made a commitment to myself that my new people and I were going to have a great time. And we got things on fire and won all the roses."

Mike had a private motivation for making the best of his demotion: he was close to the point in his career with this corporation when he would be able to retire comfortably. Still, it took courage for him to admit the failure his demotion represented, even if he had a material reason to stick with the company. It would have been very easy for him to act the victim and do only the minimum required in his new role. Faced with a similar situation, many people would have simply quit and moved on. It took courage to walk back into that office each day. He had to risk being viewed by friends and colleagues as having failed, but by taking that risk, he was able to turn this situation into a success. Even though he chose to stay with the company, he didn't have to take the high road as he did. He could have avoided those he'd worked with before and not helped the person who took his old job. What he did was very unusual and unexpected, and he surely had to overcome some embarrassment to do it.

We often say to our clients, "Ask yourself what you would do if you were 'President of the World,' as if all the people in the company were your people, and it was your job to help them become as successful as they could possibly be." Mike kept this in mind. He said that even though he was getting lots of praise for the sales organization's improving numbers, it was not nearly as difficult as it appeared to others because he had built successful relationships before both with staff and with customers, and he knew how to get results from those efforts. He didn't only rely on his previous ways of interacting, though. "My Leadership Character surveys and test results woke me up to the fact that I had a problem with authority figures. The people I worked for said basically I wasn't a team player, but my peers and the people who worked for me loved me. So I said to myself, 'I've got to be careful, given my personality, to build better rapport with the people I work for, and to keep doing what I'm doing with my peers and direct reports.'"

• • •

Taking Risks

On personality tests, some of us score very high for risk taking, and others score very low. This score tends to be more a factor of genetics than of learning, although it's obviously a combination of the two. The variations tell us that what makes it hard to act courageously can differ from person to person. Consider a person who is shy, unassuming, and low scoring for willingness to take risks. When promoted to a management position, he will be called upon to make decisions that may generate conflict. This person's natural tendency is to avoid conflict and making decisions that could create it. So it will require an effort of courage on his part to develop the necessary assertiveness skills and confidence.

On the other hand, someone who has a natural propensity toward risk taking can do something that may appear to others dangerous, or even foolhardy, without herself thinking that courage is involved. If she is bold and domineering and actually enjoys conflict, courage for her will be the willingness to do honest self-reflection and to become a more respectful leader. For either one of these people, developing balanced Leadership Character requires a willingness to be vulnerable and do something that isn't easy, though the challenges for each one are quite different.

Sometimes, just becoming more self-aware can lead to a shift in one's willingness to act with courage. During a standard life-history interview, Jorge, a division president of an international engineering firm, remarked that he was a calculated risk taker who was willing to take risks only after he had spent time evaluating the merits of the situation. But later, on his personality assessment and 360-degree review, he saw that he had scored very low on all measures of risk taking. He was astounded. He said, "I told you that I was a moderate risk taker, yet all of this shows me to be about as low as I possibly could be in risk taking."

After sitting quietly for a few minutes, Jorge took out a memo pad and began writing. When asked what he was doing, he replied, "I'm just making some notes on things I plan to do right away." A few weeks later, we received a call from his CEO, saying, "This guy has made the biggest transformation I've ever seen." The CEO said that Jorge had always been loved and respected by his people as a person of high integrity and one of the hardest workers in the company, but he was so risk averse that he would always throw cold water on new ideas. Jorge's excessive caution caused him to be indecisive and to procrastinate, but now he seemed much more assertive and confident; for example, in meetings he was not only speaking up but leading discussions.

At his next session, Jorge explained that all his life he had been censoring his own ideas because he was afraid they were too risky and foolhardy. But when he saw those graphs that showed him to be at the lowest end of the risk-taking continuum when compared to thousands of other leaders and executives, he realized that he could try almost anything he wanted to do and he wouldn't even get to the 50th percentile. If he acted on his ideas, even if he continued to think of himself as reckless, he would still probably only compare as a moderate or calculated risk taker. "I just needed to give myself permission," Jorge said. Sometimes the obstacles to acting with courage seem to be external—colleagues who might be irritated, a boss who might give a career-damaging evaluation—but Jorge's experience shows that they also reside within us, in the form of our own anxieties. His story also demonstrates that people who are extreme in any personality trait or characteristic must use conscious intention to create more balance in their behavior.

Accepting Anxiety

We all want safety. It's only human. The natural fear of vulnerability prevents many people who are working in companies or participating in organizations from seizing opportunities to provide leadership and act with integrity, even when they can clearly see what needs to be done. An action that requires courage will always create some anxiety within us. It may not feel pleasant, but this anxiety is not a negative. Rather, it is part of a positive process that is bigger than ourselves. We have to be willing to experience that anxiety to act with courage.

Courage is something we can build every day, with small gestures as well as grand ones. How often do we allow someone to gossip to us about a third person, even though it makes us uncomfortable? How willing are we to tolerate offensive jokes or racial slurs without objecting? It's awfully easy to rationalize not taking the courageous stand. We think, "She doesn't really mean any harm" or "People say this kind of thing all the time." To say instead, "I don't think that's right, and I don't want to hear it anymore," risks not only the other person's disapproval but the force of our own feelings finally being let out.

There are skills we can practice to help us be more courageous when the situation calls for it. To be more willing to take risks, we can work on building both assertiveness and confidence. To control our feelings so that they don't prohibit us from doing the right thing, we can use the Effective Self-Management techniques from chapter 4, reframing our self-talk to mitigate our anxiety.

Here are some other mental exercises that will help you build courage and integrity.

- **Imagine disaster.** When a situation calls for an act of courage, ask yourself, "What's the worst possible thing that can happen?" Imagining the very worst and figuring out how you would handle it can decrease anxiety, both because the very worst outcome is rarely the most likely and because if it does happen, it won't take you totally unprepared. For example, if you are considering giving some tough feedback to your boss, imagine that he fires you on the spot and figure out what you would do.

- **Inspire yourself.** Think of a role model, someone you really like and admire who is willing to take principled risks. Ask yourself what that person would do in the situation, and then make an assignment to yourself to do just that.

- **Think of people of courage.** Recall those who have displayed enormous courage: a corporate whistle-blower, a firefighter, a nurse in a refugee camp. Ask yourself: "What made it possible for them to do these things? How am I like them? How am I different? How can I use their example to be more courageous myself?"

- **Create a sense of obligation.** Consider what will happen to your organization if you *don't* take the initiative and do what's needed. What are the consequences of *failing* to act?

COURAGE FOR THE GREATER GOOD

Rani's Story

Rani was a manager in a large telecom company who also had extensive experience on the technical side. People saw her as honest, principled, and completely trustworthy. She was generally very strong on the qualities of respect; she made a point of building equitable relationships with others, especially those she led. Rani eagerly asked for input and shared credit; when she had a presentation to make, she would often have those who reported to her make it, so they were brought into the limelight. She was humble, never trying to take credit for herself alone. She excelled at emotional mastery and didn't let anxiety or unreasonable anger get in her way.

But Rani had some work to do on the qualities that contribute to responsibility. Although she saw herself as accountable for anything within her area, she did not see herself as personally responsible for the success of the company as a whole, nor did she see herself as able to influence the entire company. She tended to focus on her own area, even though she was interested in the success of the whole company and kept up with industry trends. Her most severe lack was courage. She had never taken the initiative to do something that would benefit the entire organization because she didn't want to displease her boss.

At the time she came to the executive development program, this posed a real challenge. Rani's boss tended to be risk averse and unsupportive of ideas that were outside the box, but Rani had realized that the company had an opportunity to develop a new product, using technology and resources already in place, that could lead to a whole new profit center. So she felt stuck and unable to

---

really use her talents and knowledge effectively for the greater good of the entire organization.

She was leery of taking this proposal to her boss for approval and seeing it rejected. Bob suggested that she first gather support outside the department, by talking about the idea with colleagues throughout the company, just to see what might evolve. Bob asked what would be the worst thing that could possibly happen. "I could get fired," Rani replied. She recognized that as unlikely, but it still took courage for her to proceed without her boss's approval. Rani had competing commitments to protect herself and stay safe, and only by appealing to her own sense of higher purpose, the success of the company, could she muster the courage to act.

"I have always tried to be loyal, in every job I've ever had," she explains now. "When Bob first suggested that I mobilize other resources within the company to pursue my idea without first running it by my own boss, it felt very risky and uncomfortable. But I really believed that this plan could benefit the company, and I decided the risk was worth it."

In a short time, because the idea was a good one, Rani had generated considerable passion and interest; she was meeting with several people from other parts of the organization at night and on weekends to develop it. When the idea evolved into a business case, Rani's boss heard about what was going on and asked her to come in. Rani did not know that her boss had recently been praised by his own superior for his department's having come up with this brilliant idea that could lead to a new source of revenue. The boss complimented Rani for having initiated it and offered the resources necessary to implement the new business case. Within a year Rani was heading up the new profit center.

In looking back, Rani could see how saying to herself, "My boss won't let me do it" was not only abdication but also in the end not true. Making her idea a reality just required some creative thinking, some risks, and courage. As she became involved in this project, she began inspiring her direct reports to take initiative and go beyond what they thought they could do. She gave them a sense of common goals and showed them what they could accomplish even without up-front management support, even in the face of obstacles. Rani realized what a tremendous amount of power and influence she had. She had focused before on what she couldn't do. Now she focused on what she could do. Her view of herself as a leader changed. She was an analytical, technical person who had not seen herself as charismatic. She was amazed to discover her power to motivate others.

• • •

It's hard to "go first" when there's something risky to be done, hard to make the ethical choice when the distinction between right and wrong can be so murky. Fear will nearly always be present when it's time to act, but you can get past anxiety by acting with courage—incrementally, in decisions small and large, every day.

Key Concepts

- Making positive change takes courage.

- Courage can mean taking personal risks for a greater good, acting despite the difficult obstacles, or being strong in the face of threats.

- Building your courage usually means learning to accept and live with anxiety.

- Good leadership requires that courage be balanced by sensitivity to the needs of others and an appreciation of the complexity of situations.

9

Self-Confidence

A t the pinnacle of his career at GE, Jack Welch said that there were three things he wanted everyone in the company to express: speed, simplicity, and self-confidence. Speed is essential because it yields a critical competitive edge, and to achieve it requires being nimble, responsive, and adaptive. Simplicity allows messages, both internal and external, to be quickly grasped and easily understood and allows systems to function with efficiency. It is easy to see the synergy of those two qualities, and also how self-confidence makes them both possible. If you're confident, you're able to step up and take responsibility, embrace necessary change, and move forward decisively. You're courageous enough to tell the truth, and straightforward in everything you do.

AN ESSENTIAL SUCCESS FACTOR

Self-confidence is an essential factor for success. "Insecure managers create complexity," Welch has said. "Real leaders don't need clutter. People must have the self-confidence to be clear, precise, to be sure that every person in their organization, highest to lowest,

———

understands what the business is trying to achieve."[1] Steve O'Brien was an officer at GE when Work-Out, the famous GE method for solving business problems by using teams of employees, was instituted. Steve, who joined our organization in 1995 after a 30-year career at GE, says Work-Out not only improved the business but dramatically increased self-confidence in all employees. "Rank-and-file employees had to develop self-confidence to present their solutions to senior managers," says Steve, "and managers had to be confident to make quick decisions on the recommendations. Managers were required to give a thumbs-up, a thumbs-down, or an 'I need more information,' and you needed really good reasons to turn the idea down or to request more information. Work-Out developed a lot of self-confident people, and confident people grow a business."

Self-confidence is important for each of us as we strive to live and act with decency—and equally important for any organization that seeks to build a culture of character. Before people can let themselves believe in a group effort and commit to it, they want to know that all members, from top to bottom, see them as playing an important role and providing leadership; that every participant, in other words, acts and interacts with self-confidence.

People will follow a person who is self-confident. Confidence helps an organization feel optimistic and forward looking. For leadership to be sustainable, though, that confidence must be balanced with relationship skills, such as humility and empathy, from the respect side of the scale. Excessive confidence without respectful social awareness comes to appear ridiculous; it's a parody of real leadership. When people see that, they sometimes say that the person has "too much self-confidence." What they are really describing, though, is arrogance. A person cannot have too much *self*-confidence because the person who is truly self-confident has no reason to behave arrogantly. Jim Collins tells a story about a conversation he once had with Admiral James Stockdale, who was a prisoner of war for eight years in Vietnam. "You must never confuse faith that you will prevail in the end (which you can never

———

afford to lose)," Stockdale told Collins, "with the discipline to confront the most brutal facts of your current reality, whatever they might be." Collins concludes that successful leadership of an enterprise requires being able to balance both optimism and realism. We would see that ability as requiring both confidence and humility.

Thinking about self-confidence makes it easy once again to see how all the essential elements that build character and enhance integrity actually complement and reinforce one another. In an earlier version of the Leadership Character Model, in fact, we placed self-confidence on the respect side of the scale. Why? Because it takes self-confidence to create equitable relationships. It takes self-confidence to see others, especially those who have formal positions of power over you, as your equals, and to tell them what you honestly think. From the opposite perspective, it takes confidence to hire people who might be smarter than you, to listen to ideas and criticism from people who are below you in the hierarchy, to open up communication in every direction and keep it flowing.

But in the end, we placed self-confidence on the responsibility platform because a factor analysis of data from our research indicated that this trait clusters most often with the other qualities on this side of the scale. We also considered the many negative possible consequences for an organization when a leader lacks this quality. An unconfident leader, when facing issues that call for decisiveness, risk taking, and courage, is likely to vacillate or simply resort to avoidance. This is particularly important when there is any urgency to the problems and in times of crisis.

Such a leader will also have trouble giving feedback others may find difficult to receive. Confidence begets confidence, so others in the organization tend not to feel inspired by a leader lacking self-confidence; individuals and the group become sapped of energy. Actually, the negative consequences of the lack of self-confidence are so many and various that they affect nearly every area of functioning and leading within an organization, including one's potential for individual advancement.

LACK OF CONFIDENCE OR LACK OF INTEREST?

Ike's Story

When Ike first entered the executive development program, he had hit a wall in his career with a regional utility company. "I had just transitioned," he remembers. "I had been managing director of marketing and had been moved into a business development group. As far as my title goes, it was a lateral move, but personally it was a demotion. Really, I'd been thrown out."

Ike had excellent technical skills and a real passion for having more influence on the direction of his company. However, he was surprised to learn that his 360-degree review respondents thought he was lacking in assertiveness and ability to take charge. He was viewed as being too cautious. "People were saying—and our CEO's comments to me, too, were—that I was not influential on issues, either up, down, or with peers. People commented that I seemed 'beaten down.' I hadn't realized it was so apparent to everybody else."

When someone's confidence is shaky, he might spend time scrambling to protect his own dignity, display a low energy level, be afraid to tell the truth or take risks, need constant reassurance, resist change, or lack confidence in his own decisions. With Ike, though, low self-esteem came out mainly as a lack of interest in the contributions of other people. "The perception was that I wasn't being assertive, but within me it was more that I just wasn't focused on influencing people. I wasn't making the effort. I alienated the rest of the team because I didn't seek their input. That's why they gave feedback that 'he's not involving us.'"

What was really going on was that because Ike felt unsure of himself as a leader, he was reluctant to make himself vulnerable by accepting other people's contributions. His experience also points to another way that a lack of self-confidence can, paradoxically, show up as arrogance. "I felt like I knew the issues better than anybody else, and so I didn't need to consult anybody; I just needed to convince everybody. The effort it took to get buy-in from large groups of people felt like a waste of time to me. I tended to have an answer before a meeting started, rather than making the meeting part of the process to come up with the solution." When that didn't work, he felt discouraged and tended to withdraw. Ike resolved to work hard on improving his self-confidence, which would in turn improve his assertiveness, decision making, risk taking, and interactions with other people.

Ike learned the concepts of Effective Self-Management, as discussed in chapter 4, and began using reframing to eliminate his old self-defeating way of thinking. Bob asked him to take stock of his assets and skill sets, to recognize his strengths. By doing this, Ike was able to begin viewing himself as more assertive and confident; with this awareness of strength, he was able both to be more passionate and to incite passion in others. The changes in his behavior were so impressive to his CEO that Ike was tapped to work on a high-level special project and subsequently urged to develop and lead a new profit center for the organization. This new confidence in Ike was affirmation of the hard work that he had done to improve his attitude and performance.

Ike says, "I've been working on—even now, I have to correct myself, because I was going to say 'getting buy-in on my ideas.' But it's not so much that as it is going into a meeting and letting the process develop the solution. When I first entered the executive development program, Bob suggested that I keep a meeting log, to evaluate myself afterwards and assess how the interaction went. I still do that. It helps me double-check to see whether I've solicited ideas. If I do that after a meeting, it helps remind me to go into the next meeting with an attitude of bringing others in. And it gives me a way to check myself, on how forthcoming and assertive I've been with my own thoughts."

• • •

CHOOSING SELF-CONFIDENCE

People often use the term *self-confidence* broadly, as if someone either has it or doesn't, but it is more accurate and useful to talk about self-confidence in relation to specific skills. The confident gourmet cook may not be a confident distance swimmer. Someone who is unfazed by setting up and maintaining a computer network may get the jitters when he has to speak in front of a group.

So it's fair to say one basis of confidence in any particular area is skill. It is impossible to perform any kind of task well until you have a firm knowledge of it and have practiced it thoroughly. Knowing that you are well prepared gives you a feeling of sureness that can't be acquired any other way. A second component of self-confidence is attitude. Once you have developed a level of competence in, say, tennis or public speaking, it would be logical to feel confident doing that thing. However, if you are competent but still lacking self-confidence in a specific area, what needs work is your attitude about that activity, or perhaps your attitude about yourself in general.

Thus when we talk about people as not having adequate self-confidence, we are usually talking about people who have developed attitudes about themselves that do not match their levels of competence. This disconnect may be rooted in childhood experiences, when they felt they could never measure up to the standards set by their parents or others around them. It may result from their own perfectionism and a tendency to set unrealistic standards in their own minds that they can never meet.

But self-confidence is there for the taking. Self-confidence is an intangible, and you can choose to have it by reframing your thinking, as long as you have developed the appropriate skills and competencies. Often it is a matter of giving yourself permission to be confident in situations where you had not been doing so. Coming to feel confident is not always this simplistic, but in many cases, by talking to themselves in this way over and over again for a period of time, people do make rapid gains in self-confidence. If having confidence is really a choice, then why not choose it?

Talking Yourself Toward Self-Confidence

Often, people find that good basic skills just aren't enough. A lawyer just out of school may have excellent legal knowledge and well-practiced speaking skills. However, he may still find himself feeling anxious and unsure before his first courtroom case. Gaining confidence requires first changing the thought patterns and the self-talk with which we intimidate ourselves about the challenging situation. Then it takes putting ourselves in the situation multiple times; exposure builds confidence and lessens the anxiety response. Many times we predict failure for ourselves; we expect the worst and then compound it by telling ourselves how terrible it will be if the worst does indeed happen. Lack of confidence naturally follows from this kind of thinking. Only a more realistic, rational self-talk can help us gain the confidence we seek.

Let's suppose that Gabriella, a high-level technical employee, has just been offered a supervisory position. She decides to take it but doesn't feel very confident about her ability to supervise. She develops a plan of action for gaining supervisory confidence. Gabriella obtains several books on management theory and supervisory techniques from a library. She also asks for leave to attend a two-day workshop designed to improve managerial skills. Yet after all this preparation, Gabriella still feels unsure. She decides to examine her thought patterns to see whether she can replace them with more productive ones.

She writes down the anxiety-producing thoughts that keep cropping up whenever she sees herself in her new position, statements such as:

- "I'm afraid I can't do this job."

- "What if the people I'll be supervising don't like me?"

- "It will be terrible if I blow this opportunity."

Gabriella then challenges each statement on her list and finds that her feeling of confidence is much greater when she deliberately replaces them with these thoughts, instead:

- "This kind of thinking doesn't help me reach my goals. I have thoroughly prepared for this, and in all probability, I will be able to do a good job. Certainly I can perform better if I'm calm and relaxed."

- "It may be reasonable to expect some initial resistance, but expecting the employees I supervise not to like me serves no purpose except to make me feel upset. It would be nice if they like me, and the odds are that they will if I show concern for them. But my first concern is to do the best job I can, and to keep the organization's best interests in balance with my employees' needs."

- "It will be unfortunate if this position doesn't work out, but telling myself that it will be terrible only makes me feel upset and anxious. If things don't go as I would like, I'll do my best to accept that calmly and find an alternative. Upsetting myself about it now would only make a bad situation worse."

This procedure can be used to develop confidence in any area. Skill development, an examination of your self-defeating thinking, and a replacement of that with more realistic ideas and a positive attitude provide an effective plan for developing your self-confidence. By repeatedly practicing the new way of thinking, you can improve your confidence over time.

Giving yourself a "stretch" assignment, that is, taking on something that feels really challenging, can help in this process. Because the activity is unfamiliar and requires you to broaden your idea of what you are capable of doing, even after mastering the necessary skill set, you might at first experience self-defeating thoughts. This just provides the opportunity for reframing, and for practicing thinking about yourself in the new, broader way. The situation that requires you to stretch can be a bit intense and stressful, but the relearning actually tends to occur quite rapidly.

———

Using Others as Models

The process of developing self-confidence is one in which you can "fake it to make it." This works at a physiological level. If you simulate the body language of confidence—a steady gaze, a solid stance—even when you're not sure you're feeling it you will feel more in charge. But if you slump your shoulders, let your gaze dart around and your hands fidget, you will look timid and anxious and feel that way, too.

Our research studies of male/female differences in leadership show that women outscore men on the majority of the leadership variables on our 360-degree review. However, one area in which women in general score significantly lower than men is self-confidence. "I had to make myself learn to do this in order to interact with executives," Lyn remembers, "and we think many women have to make a special effort in this regard. In a group, especially one dominated by men, if I remembered to meet people's gazes, stand when I needed to, and speak in a calm voice, I not only held on to my personal power; I felt confident."

GIVING AWAY HER POWER

Jennifer's Story

When Jennifer came to us, she was in an executive position in a large, highly technical Fortune 100 company. More and more women were beginning to occupy leadership positions in the company, particularly just below officer level, but in terms of upward mobility, Jennifer, though quite talented in many areas of leadership, had not gone as far as many colleagues who had started there at the same time she did. She wanted to do some self-examination to see how she might accelerate her career.

Jennifer had shown plenty of assertiveness in managing her own groups, but she was not nearly as assertive with her peers or superiors, which translated to their not seeing her as confident. On reflection, Jennifer said that being a female manager in a largely male environment probably contributed to her feeling of not measuring up. Plus, she had not had the depth of technical training and education of some of her male counterparts. Jennifer was a good example of someone who, by displaying a lack of self-confidence in certain situations, was not allowing herself to have an equal seat at the table. She was giving away her power.

"The 360-degree feedback gave me a positive feeling," she says now. "My team thought very highly of me and had great respect for me. So did my clients and supervisors. That gave me a boost. So I started trying to emulate those people who have self-confidence, to be more observant and see what they do with it. Today, when I address a group of people or try to coach or develop people, I'm much more aware of my own strengths and weaknesses, of the tools that I can use, the kinds of things to say. It's about awareness, keeping things at the top of your mind. Often, awareness is all I need to make improvements."

• • •

As Jennifer discovered, it can be very useful to pay attention to how successful, powerful people conduct themselves, and to use those people as models. We can't think of anyone who personifies self-confidence better than Nelson Mandela. As the leader of South Africa's remarkable transition from the repressive, white-ruled apartheid state to the pluralistic, multiracial democracy of today, Mandela certainly expressed many essential aspects of integrity. During the twenty-seven years he was held in jail for his anti-apartheid organizing, for example, he always treated his captors with courtesy, while keeping his own dignity and authority. He obviously had the emotional mastery to transcend his own frustrating, perhaps frightening, situation, and to keep the larger picture in mind. Mandela had the empathy to know that change would depend on overcoming whites' fears. "It was a shock to meet these [black] people and see that they were intelligent human beings," one of his white prison wardens later recalled. "Mr. Mandela was a prisoner but also a leader, anybody could see that. . . . The moment he walked into a room, his manner, his way of speaking, his dress, you knew he was a leader."[2]

"Among leaders, they come no stronger than Nelson Mandela," Patti Waldmeir wrote in *Anatomy of a Miracle*, her account of the country's transition to democracy. "Partly, this dominance is physical, the effect, simply, of a tall man who stands up very straight. But it is more than that." Mandela had come from tribal aristocracy, and his bearing and self-consciousness always reflected that. "Mandela was born to rule. He thinks so, and after a few moments, so do you."[3]

Using Yourself as a Model

Two other effective techniques for building self-confidence rely on using yourself as a model. One involves role-playing. With another person, have a conversation about an upcoming situation that you anticipate will be stressful and that might find you feeling unconfident. Talk through the experience as you expect it to go. Don't filter yourself, but do listen to yourself. Then reframe your ideas about how you will conduct yourself, in the way that Gabriella did in the earlier example. Now role-play the situation again, this time purposefully talking from a confident point of view. Hearing yourself talk about it from both perspectives helps you distance yourself somewhat from the feelings and creates an objectivity that allows you to grow faster.

The other technique involves positive visioning: seeing yourself functioning successfully in a situation you find challenging. An experience we had with our sons, when Rob was nine and Josh was five, shows how effective this can be. We had spent two days in a continuing education workshop on hypnosis; it was a credible presentation that consisted mostly of focused attention techniques to accelerate growth in a particular area. At supper that Sunday evening, after hearing us talking excitedly about our workshop, Rob said, "Dad, why don't you hypnotize me so I can hit a home

———

run? I've never hit one." Then Josh piped up. "Yeah, Dad. Hypnotize me, too, so I can hit a home run, too, 'cause I've never hit a home run before either." Josh was playing tee ball at the time, which is baseball without a pitcher. The ball is placed on a tee about chest high. Rob was playing standard baseball.

So that night, and every subsequent night that week, Bob went into each of their rooms and spent about 15 minutes, just prior to their going to sleep. Bob remembers, "I would say to Josh, 'You're feeling very, very relaxed, but you're not going to sleep yet. Now picture a scene where you feel the most comfortable. At the lake? At the beach? Just keep picturing that and feeling relaxed and comfortable. Now switch the scene to the baseball field. Picture yourself at the batter's box. Picture yourself holding the bat the way we practice, and now swinging the bat, and keeping your eye on the ball, on the tee, as your bat makes contact. Now picture the ball sailing over the second baseman's head. See yourself running to first base. You are running faster than you've ever run before. You see yourself rounding first, rounding second, rounding third, and sliding into home plate. You have just hit a home run.' I repeated this sequence several times within a 15-minute time frame.

"Then I would go to Rob's room and say exactly the same thing, except that for Rob, because he had a pitcher instead of a tee, I would say, 'Now you see yourself standing in the batter's box with the bat back, the way we practice. See the pitcher wind up with the ball. See the ball coming out of his hand. See it come all the way to where you swing and make contact with it. Now see it flying over the second baseman's head.'" Rob had his game that Friday night. He hit his first home run. The next morning, Josh had his tee ball game. He hit two home runs, one a grand slam. "I was swamped by their teammates," Bob laughs. "They were clamoring, 'Dr. Turknett, Dr. Turknett—hypnotize *me* to hit a home run!'"

Since those days, visualization and techniques for focused attention have become commonplace, both in sports and for eliminating bad habits or developing new good ones. It only takes a quick Internet search to turn up numerous studies that support the notion that these techniques can accelerate the development of competence and confidence. Actually, we all use these techniques

———

frequently in our lives but are usually unaware that we are doing so. By intentionally using techniques like visualization to help ourselves relearn and reframe, we can accelerate our mastery of specific skills and build our confidence.

Building Confidence in Yourself and Others

If you are a manager, developing strengths in the people who report to you should be one of your main responsibilities, but it's not unusual for a manager who lacks confidence to do that poorly. Ike, for instance, whose lack of self-confidence prevented him from engaging other people in the problem-solving process, was also weak in coaching them. "I got a lot of feedback on my 360 that I did not address personnel issues: giving praise and recognition, holding people accountable," Ike recalls. "I got comments that I didn't hold other people to the same standard that I set for myself. It's still not natural for me," he says. "It requires me to have it as a goal to look at almost daily. I have to remind myself to talk to people and pat them on the back. You have to recognize your shortcomings and then work on those."

Increasing the confidence of those you manage helps build organizations that can are confident and proactive. The ideas we use to build self-esteem in the leaders we work with can be used in turn to build self-confidence in direct reports and others. These are some of the approaches we take with our clients, and that we encourage them to use with others.

- We view them positively.

- We treat them with respect.

- We work to find common ground with them.

- We initiate conversation and then listen.

- We help them feel competent by pointing out their strengths.

- We give honest feedback, without surprises.

- We show vulnerability and humility ourselves.

These are the attitudes to take in treating people with decency. Leaders can and should reflect these in the workplace, along with other confidence-building gestures like asking those they lead for ideas and advice, asking them to articulate what support they need, and sharing information. The point of doing this is to help individuals feel strong by recognizing their real strengths and, in turn, through them to strengthen organizations.

Key Concepts

- Self-confidence involves taking responsibility, embracing necessary change, and moving forward decisively.

- Self-confidence is an essential quality for a leader. People will follow a person who is self-confident.

- Learning to be more self-confident can be achieved through positive self-talk, taking on "stretch" assignments, finding role models, role-playing, and positive visioning.

- Leadership effectiveness requires that self-confidence be balanced with humility and empathy. Good leaders also build self-confidence in others.

10

Focus on the Whole

Of the four qualities that make up responsibility, focus on the whole is the one that best reveals a person's maturity and resilience. It is also the one most essential to leading at the highest levels. To focus on the whole means to see one's particular situation in its larger context and at the same time to remain aware of how both the particular situation and its larger context are always evolving.

At the most basic level, for an individual contributor, focusing on the whole means keeping the perspective of the larger organization constantly in view, rather than the more limited perspective of your own job, area, or department. We often use this question to challenge people to broaden their perspective, and to see how their own behavior impacts the larger system: "What factors about your department would, if true, cause problems for the rest of the organization?" Focus on the whole is necessary in order to expand your notion of responsibility, to truly take responsibility for the larger enterprise. As people mature as leaders, the whole they perceive as important naturally expands to include the industry, the economic environment, the political situation, and so on.

It is common nowadays to acknowledge that the only constant in life is change. This is certainly true in business. Economic and political conditions, technologies, and demographics are all continually in flux. As business moves faster and becomes more globally linked, the whole we need to understand grows larger, more ambiguous, and more complex. Sometimes, in response, organizations must go as far as shifting the very ways they do business. At a time when, for example, firms willingly form alliances with their competitors, the ability to see with the widest perspective, to perceive the real conditions and systems that are in operation, becomes critical. This can feel bewildering or it can feel exhilarating. That just depends on how you think about yourself in relation to growth and change. It is in considering the problem of how to grow people's focus on the whole that we refer for inspiration to *kokoro*, the Japanese Buddhist idea of the ever-expanding and maturing character, mentioned in the discussion of seeing yourself as dynamic and always growing, in chapter 1.

In Japanese culture, the mindfulness of *kokoro* is applied in circumstances as various as the traditional tea ceremony, the practice of martial arts, the design of gardens, and, systematically, the nurturing of corporations. With *kokoro*, as one follower put it, "We let go of our emotional attachment to other information we have been exposed to, so that we might listen more carefully and digest what we will hear in the future." A similar balance of detachment and engagement characterizes a focus on the whole. That balance allows two things at once: perspective and nimble response.

This balance between detached reflection and engagement is very well expressed by a concept developed by Ronald Heifetz, called "achieving a balcony perspective." In the book Heifetz coauthored with Marty Linsky, *Leadership on the Line,* the authors imagine a ballroom filled with dancers. "The only way you can gain both a clearer view of reality and some perspective on the bigger picture is by distancing yourself from the fray,"[1] by overlooking the crowded room from a raised vantage point. "To see yourself from the outside as merely one among the many dancers, you have to watch the system and the patterns, looking at yourself as part of the overall scheme. You must set aside your special knowledge of your intentions and inner feelings, and notice that part of yourself that others would see if they were looking down from the balcony."[2] That was the challenge for our client Beverly.

ACCEPTING CONFLICT AND FOSTERING CREATIVITY

Beverly's Story

Beverly had recently been promoted to executive vice president in a large public utility company that faced enormous challenges. When she came to the executive development program, not only had the industry been deregulated but there was new top management in place. The organization's imperative was to transform itself from slow and bureaucratic to agile and entrepreneurial. Beverly had excellent people and communication skills, and plenty of drive. What she needed most was to alter her view of herself from someone who was running an area of the company to someone who was taking responsibility for the entire organization—to learn the skills of management at a higher level. A big piece of that, when you are in an EVP role in a large organization, is seeing yourself as leading the entire organization, even if you are responsible only for certain functional areas, and even though everyone doesn't report up through you. For Beverly, that demanded learning to think more strategically and learning to approach contention and change more effectively.

"I have about 150 people who report up through me," she says. "I had to figure out ways to keep in touch with the reality at all the different levels without getting sucked into it. In upper-level management, a lot of your position is dealing with conflict. To work through it takes a shift in methodology. You leave behind personalities. You set aside anything other than facts. You just get down to the details and break them out, analyze the pieces.

"When you get into upper management, there are lots of egos, and we all come into situations with preconceived ideas. Being able to manage through that, to get to where you want to go, is significant and difficult. I've learned to step back and dissect things and approach conflict in an organized way." What allows Beverly to maintain such perspective, even in times of turmoil and transition? Attention to the interconnections and influence patterns between the individual and the group, and between the parts and the whole.

• • •

We might be inclined to think highly of a manager who takes pride in protecting his team from politics and conflicts, but what consequences might that kind of thinking actually have? Theoretically, this leader could eke out very good results from his team while the company is busy going out of business. This manager may see himself as a leader and agent of change, but by protecting his people, he prevents them from making their best contributions to the betterment of the organization—and unwittingly enables a sense of separation.

Focusing on the whole, however, he would want to equip his leaders, through coaching and development opportunities, with the skills and resources needed for them to see how their work enhances the entire organization and helps create its success. He would want to convey to everyone an understanding of the business as a whole and generate enthusiasm for the company's goals. He would ensure that information about financial results, competitive pressures, key drivers, and the like is widely available, so everyone feels involved in the company's decisions. Fostering a sense of connectedness would be seen as an important way to unleash the creative energy that is potential within the organization, a way to help the organization itself be more alert and responsive. He would help them all, in other words, take part in the leadership of the organization. "Leadership," in the words of theorist William Drath, "is a property of a social system, an outcome of collective meaning-making, not the result of influence or vision from an individual . . . leaders and followers alike participate in leadership."[3]

Remember David, the former military officer, whom we described in chapter 6? He worked to develop humility by learning the skill of active listening. His responsibility was for the internal travel agency at a major telecommunications company, buying services from hotel and car rental chains, airlines and other large vendors. As David developed his Leadership Character by working to respect others more, his sense of responsibility for the whole corporation grew, as did his grasp of the direction of the entire organization. He began to see that he could leverage the business he gave those vendors, who could be big customers for his company's services, so he brought them together with his firm's salespeople. David became the catalyst for several million-dollar-plus deals because he paid attention to the whole enterprise, not just to his own part of it.

CONSTRUCTIVE DEVELOPMENTAL THEORY

Robert Kegan, a Harvard University professor of adult learning and professional development, has a powerful and inspiring theory of the stages of maturity. Kegan's theoretical perspective has proved to be especially useful when applied to the character development needed by leaders and has added depth to our own work. Called Constructive Developmental Theory, it is a model of adult development based on the idea that human beings naturally progress over a lifetime through as many as five distinct stages.[4]

At the first order of consciousness, or stage one, the very young child has not yet formulated the idea of a permanent, separate self. The person at stage two is typically a child or young adolescent, who understands being differentiated from others but still pursues mainly selfish goals. At stage two a person can't take the perspective of the other and is driven only by his or her own needs.

Stage three development should come in late adolescence or early adulthood, though it sometimes doesn't, causing major problems. People at stage three are fully socialized adults, who look to others (the community, family, the organization) as sources of values and self-worth. They recognize that others have different points of view and can empathize with others. But they are enmeshed in the roles and relationships around them and tend to avoid conflict for fear that it will lead to the loss of esteem either for themselves or for others.

With growth to stage four, individuals have developed a value system that is truly theirs, a strong, individualized point of view that is self-authored. They have mastered an important skill of balance: they can see and empathize with others, but they can do this from an outside perspective. They have developed their views about the world and recognize their own power in having done so. Individuals at stage four are responsible in the truest sense; they understand the power they have to create their own feelings and responses. They understand the source of their own and others' values. They are much better able to deal with conflict; they aren't dependent on others for their self-esteem. They are, at this stage, able to commit to an institution or organization without being engulfed or overwhelmed by it; they can be a part of a group without being dependent on it. They can move beyond self-blame and blaming others to claim the power to step outside themselves, observe the situation, and be a force for change. They are the authors of their own lives.

At stage five, which many of us don't reach, people can even see the limits of their own value systems. As leaders, people at stage five are most open to ambiguities, most able to perceive and hold polarities in tension, and most concerned with larger systems—not just the corporation, but the country, or the world. They are most able to focus on the whole. At stage four an individual has developed a strong, resilient, self-aware ego. At stage five the individual has fully developed the humility and expanded consciousness to move beyond ego.

Kegan and others have collected data over the years on the developmental stage of thousands of adults. The data show that most adults, even those in professional or leadership positions in organizations, are primarily at stage three or between stages three and four, not at stage four or five.

Karl Kuhnert, a professor of psychology at the University of Georgia and senior research fellow at Turknett Leadership Group,

———

and his colleague, Keith Eigel, report research findings that board-elected CEOs and presidents of successful public firms with over $1 billion in revenue are at higher levels of development than those in lower levels or in management at less successful firms.[5] At the most successful firms, leaders were at levels four and five only.

Growth to the next level is generally understood to be spurred by critical events, or, as Kuhnert and Eigel put it, "When new experiences contradict our current ways of understanding ourselves, others, and our situations, then those contradictory experiences become the fuel for development."[6] We believe that such transitions can be accelerated through intentional feedback, challenges to established patterns of thinking, and support. Working with our executive clients, we find that people can be brought to recognize the limitations of their stage three thinking and behavior, and with their new awareness and much work, purposefully make a shift to the next level of leadership.

People want to move forward. The framework of Constructive Developmental Theory facilitates the growth process because it motivates people to challenge their own thinking. It provides a model of how to lead powerfully that is simultaneously self-conscious and selfless. During their videotaped life-history interviews, participants in our executive development program are asked, "How would you like to be remembered?" Most have responded that they want to make a difference in the world. The aspiration to express decency and integrity in some lasting way is present in nearly everyone, but the level of development most have attained does not yet enable them to attain that goal.

Given that Kegan's data show that most people working in organizations have a level of development below the level needed to focus on the betterment of the institution, it follows that many leaders in our government and leaders of other nations are operating at a level below that needed to focus on the betterment of the institution they are responsible for. For them, soberingly, the institution in question might be thought of as the entire planet or all of human civilization, and only at stage five would leaders be capable of focusing so broadly. These data certainly suggest the urgency of fostering growth in consciousness and character in all people who are in organizations, and, for that matter, in all people. The prospect for the beneficial resolution of conflicts will be very different if we have leaders with a spirit of decency and the ability to maintain an awareness of the biggest picture—the needs of all humanity—rather than leaders concerned primarily with their own interests or the singular interests of their teams, companies, tribes, or nations.

Each of us can make a positive difference in the world, through the consciousness we bring to bear on all the moment-to-moment decisions of life, big and small. Every interaction is a chance to add more respect, responsibility, and integrity to the world. People who push themselves to reach a higher level of maturity, developing Leadership Character and all the qualities and skills it is built from, can do that in the most strategic and effective ways. They create a heritage of decency. Though this may be a spiritual or cultural legacy rather than a tangible one, it will be extended and renewed every time anyone touched by it also chooses to act with integrity. Thus, its potential real impact on the world is unlimited.

EMBRACING POLARITIES

"The true test of a first-rate mind," wrote F. Scott Fitzgerald, "is the ability to hold two contradictory opinions at the same time." Focus on the whole requires the ability to let opposites coexist: to embrace polarities. In a polarity, two seemingly opposed forces (needs, desires, or possible paths of action) are recognized, valued, and maintained in balance. Linguistically, to embrace polarities we have to construct our thinking using "both/and" rather than "either/or."

Barry Johnson, author of *Polarity Management*, uses the analogy of breathing.[7] You can't concentrate only on inhaling or only on exhaling; breathing is a natural example of balancing polarities. In organizations, there are many polarities that must be balanced: respect and responsibility; structure and flexibility; stability and change; short-term gain and long-term viability; centralization and decentralization; cost and quality. Johnson thinks some organizations misread polarity challenges as problems to be solved by choosing one side over the other. But a decision, say, that decentralization is the wave of the future would be as silly and one-sided as a decision that in the future we need only inhale.

Within the Leadership Character Model, the polarity of respect and responsibility has to be embraced in order to lead with character and integrity. Another polarity that concerns us especially is that of ethical concerns versus financial concerns. A decent organization cannot relegate ethics to the task list of the legal department, or to the agenda of an annual executive-team retreat. Leaders and organizations that strive for integrity can no more put ethical concerns aside than they can put financial concerns aside. With this polarity, it must be "both/and" at all times.

THE MATURITY FACTOR: "MEMORIES OF THE FUTURE"

Focus on the whole is probably the most difficult quality of responsibility to develop, and it is especially elusive for young managers. It is directly related to maturity and to the body of experience and expectation that we as living organisms accumulate and nurture over time. Few books better describe both the expanded perceptions and the strategic abilities a senior leader needs than *The Living Company* by Arie de Geus, one of the originators of scenario planning.[8] De Geus was at Shell for thirty-four years and moved into the planning department, an area held in high regard at that company, only after managing large operations for a number of years.

While in the planning role, De Geus studied companies that had survived for hundreds of years. He discovered that they managed for survival as much as for profit and did so just as any successful organism manages for survival, by constantly learning and adapting. In his view, the metaphor of company as machine, while efficient in a stable economy, lulls us into managing only for the present and leaves us ill-prepared for coping with an ever-changing environment. De Geus studied the work of neurobiologist David Ingvar and concluded that it's more useful in facing the future to treat companies, like individuals, as living organisms, and to develop, as living organisms do, complex and multiple "memories of the future." Memories of the future are possible scenarios and resulting possible paths of action. In this thinking, a living company is a learning enterprise, not just an economic enterprise. Focusing on the whole—being able to play out a range of scenarios—helps companies react and evolve because they are used to thinking flexibly about what might occur.

Though this process mostly occurs unconsciously, we human beings as living organisms are constantly constructing scenarios to help us act in the future. We are continually sorting experiences and signals from our environments, to create hypotheses and anticipate consequences. "If x happens, then I will do y." The more options for the future we have worked out, the more "if, then" scenarios we store up, the better we are able to respond effectively.

Twenty years ago, the two of us were deep in conversation in a pizza place. The server brought us mugs of beer. When Lyn picked hers up to take a sip, she splashed it all over herself. "I saw the mug and unconsciously calculated the force I needed to lift it, but in my experience until then, beer mugs were made of glass. I had just encountered my first plastic one! But as a living organism, I quickly expanded my idea of what is possible in a beer mug, and now, with barely a conscious thought, I find myself testing for the weight of plastic or glass whenever I pick one up for the first time. I had developed numerous memories of the future for picking up cups and glasses: I had already experienced, and in an unconscious way planned for, Styrofoam coffee cups, lead crystal goblets, bone china teacups, stoneware mugs—and all without a thought. But I had no previous experience of plastic mugs, and without an accurate memory of the future, you can't respond appropriately." But now, one beer-splattered blouse later, Lyn had developed a memory of the future: an idea of what could happen, based on what had happened.

Of course, to build memories of the future within organizations, we must vastly increase our understandings: of the systems we operate within; of economic forces, industry trends, and new technologies; of all the environmental forces and conditions that are relevant to our future. Paradoxically, sometimes this means continuing in our current business while we invent a future in which that activity is no longer relevant. As we write this, for example, Polaroid has almost disappeared, its self-developing photo technology rendered obsolete by one-hour developing. Now the film industry, so long dominated by Kodak, is being superseded by the technology of digital photography, which Kodak obviously foresaw too dimly. Rather than generating multiple, robust memories of the future based on an exquisite sensitivity to their environments and developing multiple plans for response, de Geus would suggest that these companies, like many others, more likely have been trying to *predict* the future, by extrapolating from the past. That usually narrows down expectations of what might happen to a single possibility, upon which we proceed to make elaborate plans. Then we find ourselves blindsided by the actual, unpredictable future and its surprising complexities.

Focus on the whole is hard to attain, but you can stretch yourself and develop this leadership quality with these exercises in thinking and planning.

- **Develop scenarios for the future of your industry.** To do this, you need to become extremely knowledgeable about the prevailing conditions surrounding your enterprise. Read the general business press *(Fortune, Forbes, The Wall Street Journal)* and any relevant industry- or region-specific business publications. Once you have filled out the details of your landscape, do an environmental analysis of it. Ask what's happening that may affect your industry and company, in technology, politics and government, general economic conditions, customer demographics and changes. What might all this mean? Where might your industry be in five years? Ten years?

- **Develop a strategic plan for yourself, your department, and your company.** Before you begin, read (or reread) some of the provocative books on business strategy and organizational success that we list in the Notes section at the end of the book. Start with a broad vision of the future for your industry, based on the environmental analysis you did in your scenario planning. Where would you like to be in three years? Five years? A strategic plan answers the question, "What can we do to get there?" Break this down into its components: What markets, products, and so on should you focus on? What tactics should you use? How will you measure your success? How will you allow for and adapt to the changes you cannot predict?

- **Think of yourself as the president.** Imagine that you are the president of your organization, or even of the world. Your job is to help every other person to be the most successful person he or she can be. You never make a decision without thinking about how it will affect your entire organization. If everyone in the company takes this attitude and has this underlying requirement regardless of his or her job or position, what kind of company could this be? What a difference this attitude would make in people's approaches to conflicts and decisions! What would happen to the self-interest and politics-playing that motivate so much of what goes on? Most of our clients who try this approach for several weeks report that they see significant differences in both productivity and the performance of the people they have influenced with it, and an equally significant expansion of their own vision.

- **Develop a Force Field Analysis for your department, your organization, and your industry.** First developed by pioneering social psychologist Kurt Levin, Force Field Analysis is a technique for looking at any situation, goal, or proposal for the future in terms of *driving forces* and *restraining forces*. Driving forces are trends, impulses, and conditions that help you reach your goal or make a proposed change more likely to happen. For example, if you are thinking of changing careers, driving forces might include that you find your work boring and dislike the work location. Restraining forces are those that would keep you from reaching your goal or make change less likely. In the career change example, you might be restrained by the fact that your salary is high and your husband doesn't want to move. Use Exercise 2 to guide you through the process.

EXERCISE 2

Force Field Analysis

Action or change being considered: _____

A Force Field Analysis can be used as a tool to think globally and strategically about any planned action or change. You can use this technique to analyze such changes as career transition, a new product launch, a work group consolidation, a software implementation, a merger, or a decision to outsource.

How do YOU personally evaluate the change? What are your thoughts and feelings about the change? What benefits might it bring? What problems would it solve? What problems would it create? Describe thoughts both in favor and against.

What are the broad implications of the change? Consider organizational impact, impact on external partners, impact on industry, impact on strategy, etc.

What are the driving (positive) forces? List all forces driving the change or action. Driving forces are conditions or trends that will work for change. Rate the strength of each from 1 (weak) to 5 (strong). You may also give each an importance rating from 1 to 5.

What are the restraining (negative) forces? List all restraining forces working against the change or action. These are forces that will inhibit the change or make it more difficult. Rate the strength of each from 1 (weak) to 5 (strong). You may also give each an importance rating from 1 to 5.

Examine the list of driving and restraining forces. Sum the strength and importance ratings for the driving forces and for the restraining forces. Do the positives overpower the negatives or vice versa?

If you move forward, how will you handle each of the restraining forces?

—

"WHEN IT'S TIME, I'LL BE READY"

Art's Story

Art was the vice president of sales for an international neuro-science company. His superiors were interested in grooming him for advancement, but though he was good on the respect side of the scale, he needed to develop his "sense of presence," including self-confidence, formal speaking abilities, and willingness to take charge. To make the necessary changes, Art would also need to show more courage in taking risks and in making decisions that weren't always so popular but were in the best interest of the company. Most of all, he needed to improve his focus on the whole and his ability to always keep the big picture in mind.

This transformation required him to take a new perspective on conflict. "Conflict with customers was no problem," he recalls, "but internal conflict I tended to avoid." In terms of self-change, Art is one of the most passionate clients we have ever worked with. He quickly learned the concepts in Effective Self-Management and used reframing frequently to think in a new way regarding self-confidence. He took courses in public speaking and also used reframing to eliminate some of the negative self-talk that he had previously engaged in prior to giving a speech. He was especially motivated to improve on conflict management. "I wanted to get to the bottom of it and see what I was avoiding," he says. "That was mostly my perception of what the outcomes could be, telling myself that people might be angry if I didn't make decisions in their favor. But what really happened about this for me was much more: I learned the ability to take a distance from conflict, look at it objectively, and not get emotionally drawn in.

"Understanding about the developmental levels has given me a new view of the company, rather than of my department and my functions. I'm much more inclined now to work with people at all levels to look at the way things are going within the business, and the way we and they could do things better. I also have a much keener awareness of people at all levels in the organization now, and I can see when something pops up. A year ago I would have said, 'That's their business, I'm going to focus on what I'm doing.' Now I think, 'OK, here's a potential for someone to learn or grow.' I look at that in terms of my other priorities and think, 'Maybe I could do something here.' And maybe it takes five minutes, or maybe it takes an hour, or maybe I say, 'This isn't the right time; I'll just have to let this one pass.'"

As his confidence and perceptiveness continued to increase, Art became a much stronger contributor to the company as a whole. He had always been very effective in running his own department but he was now being viewed as helping to lead the company with its new vision. Art can see that if he continues the acceleration in his growth, it will not be very long before he will be ready to become president of the organization.

"When I play tennis, I can picture in my mind going out there and playing and winning," he says. "But the presidency is a role I haven't had yet so I find it hard at this point to picture myself in that scene, and what I'd be doing there. I think I need to define myself a little more in my own mind. I don't yet feel totally confident. But I'm learning and developing. And while I may not sit in the president's chair now, I can still take on those sorts of responsibilities and work with people from that perspective, so that when it's time, I'll be ready."

• • •

An ability to focus on the whole is the single trait that most clearly distinguishes those who are mature in consciousness from those who are mature only in years. It's the quality that most clearly separates good leaders from great ones. The more you learn to do it, the more powerful and satisfied you will be.

Key Concepts

- Focus on the whole means keeping the perspective of the larger organization constantly in view.

- Focusing on the whole also requires being able to embrace polarities.

- Focus on the whole becomes more important as you rise in a leadership hierarchy; it is the quality that most separates great leaders from good ones.

- The capacity to focus on the whole can be enhanced by building future memories, doing force field analyses, developing industry analyses and strategic plans, and imagining yourself in the top role.

Integrity at Work, and All the Time

Barbara Reilly, who teaches organizational behavior at Georgia State University and works with us as a senior consultant and executive coach, tells a story about a graduate student with whom she had been considering taking on a joint research project. One morning, when they were on the way into a coffee shop for a breakfast meeting, Barbara stopped to buy a newspaper from a coin box. "Wait," the student said. "While you have it open, let me just get one, too." That small incident told Barbara all she needed to know. There was no way she would enter into the joint project after that.

It's hard to ignore big, glaring ethical dilemmas, like the applicant who is obviously passed over for a job because of race or gender, or the deposit you didn't make that appears in your account due to a bank error. But we often don't realize how our integrity is challenged in small, subtle ways as well as large ones, all the time. We also frequently underestimate how difficult it is to know what's actually right in a situation. These things are as true for our organizations as they are for us as individuals. Doing the right thing, and keeping behavior consistent with values, takes consciousness and commitment we must renew every day.

_____

INTEGRITY: THE PLACE YOU START AND THE PLACE YOU FINISH

Integrity is the most basic attribute of character. It is authenticity, knowing who you are and what you stand for, and being willing to let others know it too. Integrity is also honesty, being willing to tell the truth, even when that's painful or difficult. Integrity is developed by ethical choice; to build it, you must be able to recognize ethical choices when they arise, reason your way through them, and stick to your convictions and decisions.

Leaders must have not only integrity but also a *reputation* for integrity. Acting with respect and responsibility is critical for developing one. Leaders with integrity *walk the talk.* They model their ethics every day and make certain their actions and ideals are visible and known. There's convincing evidence that management with integrity has a positive effect on the bottom line. In a study of Holiday Inn hotels reported in the *Harvard Business Review,* researchers found that the greater the number of positive responses employees gave to such items as, "My manager delivers on promises" and "My manager practices what he preaches," the more profitable the hotel.[1]

Many leaders have a tough time being honest and forthcoming. Often, they think they are doing the people in the workforce a favor by protecting them from difficult circumstances. They might withhold troubling information or in other ways allow the differentials of power and position to create distance and filter communication. In today's workforce, which is full of highly educated people who have instant access to vast amounts of information, this kind of behavior breeds cynicism and distrust. Authenticity in leadership demands removing the mask, making yourself present, and telling the truth. A recent article in *Business Week* about Jack Stack, who successfully practiced and preached open-book management at Springfield Remanufacturing, extended the notion of corporate transparency beyond the issue of financial transparency to investors and pointed out how an ethical enterprise must also be transparent to its employees.[2] Stack believes that building a company is more important than turning out a product, and that sharing all information, including all financials, builds mutual trust and high levels of commitment and loyalty. In this book, you've seen the effect practicing these ideals has had on real leaders who have committed to them in real life.

Robert Kegan's ideas about the stages of adult development (discussed in the preceding chapter) are right on the mark when it comes to integrity. It's difficult for a person to have solid integrity without having developed the center and the perspective that stage four implies. At stage four, you have a value system that is truly yours and that you can hold on to, no matter what. People who have not yet reached stage four certainly have values, but they tend to be too dependent on what surrounds them. They are too concerned with what others think, deriving their sense of themselves through identification with a group, whether that's a workplace, a social network, or even a religion. Stage three is the home of the true believer, and the true believer is a follower. At stage four, the beliefs you hold are really yours; they form a rock-solid base for integrity and leadership.

RESPECT AND RESPONSIBILITY: BALANCE AT THE CORE

The Leadership Character concepts discussed in this book all support integrity. Integrity is a quality to focus on separately, but it is reinforced and enhanced by developing those other qualities of character, and particularly by achieving a dynamic balance of respect and responsibility. Though the Leadership Character Model was developed from our work with leaders and on the basis of empirical data, and the terms *respect* and *responsibility* are particularly apt in the context of organizational and social interaction, seeing behavior as a polarity is nothing new. Polarity and balance are at the core of all the concepts of character we know of, no matter how diverse the cultures they arise from.

One of the most ancient expressions of this polarity is the Taoist conception of yin and yang. In Taoism, yin and yang are the two properties into which the universe is divided. Yang represents the principles of masculinity: heaven, agency, dominance, control, creation, light, heat, hardness, and so on. Yin includes the principles of femininity: earth, communion, completion, receptivity, submission, darkness, coolness, softness. Yang is analogous to responsibility; yin is analogous to respect. All the opposites in the universe can be conceptually reduced to one or the other of these two opposing forces. Change comes about through the continual flow of one principle into the other. Yin is produced from yang, and yang is produced from yin in an eternal cycle. They complete each other. Living in harmony means keeping these forces in balance.

Cognitive linguist George Lakoff points out that our conception of liberal and conservative is also an expression of this same basic polarity.[3] In his book *Moral Politics*, Lakoff suggests that the liberal ideal is based on a *nurturant parent* family model, emphasizing respect, while the conservative ideal is that of a *strict father* family, emphasizing responsibility. In his book *A Brief History of Everything*, Ken Wilber talks about the cultural imperative to balance the male, yang, responsibility principle with the female, yin, respect principle. "Nature did not split the human race into two sexes for no reason; simply trying to make them the same seems silly. But even the most conservative theorists would acknowledge that our culture has been predominantly weighted to the male value sphere for quite some time now. And so we are in the delicate, dicey, very difficult, and often rancorous process of trying to balance the scales a bit more. Not erase the differences, but balance them."[4]

Recognizing the existence of polarity within each of us— between yin and yang, male and female, respect and responsibility— is a challenge. It is also, as we have seen, a mark of maturity and Leadership Character. In many aspects of our society, there is now an impetus to reach a better balance by enhancing the female principle. For leadership, too, there has been a recognition of the necessity and usefulness of developing respect. But while we are among those who seek to foster this side of our individual characters and of our culture, we are also deeply concerned at the trend toward abdication of responsibility. Remember the woman who sued McDonald's after she spilled hot coffee in her lap? She's become the archetype for abdicating responsibility. Even though there's evidence that her case was better founded than most of us realize, the incident itself seems to have led to even more frivolous lawsuits. For example, McDonald's settled a lawsuit from another woman claiming to have suffered second-degree burns from a pickle. America is the world's most litigious society, and that reflects a disturbingly widespread mentality of victimhood and lack of personal responsibility. To argue for and build the qualities of respect is not to argue against and undermine the qualities of responsibility. It's not either/or; it's both/and.

LEADING WITH ETHICS: THE LETTER AND THE SPIRIT

Most companies have an established code of conduct, but an ethical code is not sufficient to create ethical people or an ethical organization. Enron, after all, had a written code in which integrity was a stated value. A code must be made to live in the consciousness of an organization; the code must be its conscience.

An explicit code may not be sufficient, but it is still necessary. The code should be a statement of values that is both clear and inspiring. Those values should be supported by specific practices that are developed with input and support from everyone in the organization and they should answer questions like these: What constitutes a conflict of interest in this organization? How will we view and treat our customers? What do we owe to our community?

Beyond the simple drafting of this overarching code of ethics, however, discussion of its values and commitment to them should be undertaken in every part of an organization. The questions then become more practical and specific: How will our sales contracts be written? How will procurement treat suppliers? What will happen when specifications are not quite met in manufacturing? You can't act with integrity if you're making decisions without an ethical basis. Values must inform your everyday decisions.

Kenneth Cloke and Joan Goldsmith, in their book *The End of Management and the Rise of Organizational Democracy*, suggest a wonderful list of questions that can help connect decisions to values.[5] Asking them and answering honestly, about both the small and the large choices you face, will help you develop and exercise integrity.

- *Significance*—What values are at play in this decision?

- *Universality*—What would happen if everyone did what I am about to do?

- *Leadership*—What would happen if no one did what I am about to do?

- *Reciprocity*—How would I feel if the same standard were applied to me?

- *Publicity*—How would I feel if my actions were made public?

- *Defensibility*—How easy would it be to justify the action to others?

- *Responsibility*—Am I willing to take responsibility for the action or inaction, no matter what the outcome?

- *Intuition*—Does the action feel right or wrong to me?

- *Legacy*—Am I willing for my children to live with the consequences of my action or inaction?

The Difficulty of Recognizing What's Right

Life is full of nuance and contradiction. People are pulled by competing values, commitments, and loyalties and struggle to act on them. It's rarely easy to arrive at a certain knowledge of the right thing to do. Suppose, for example, the poor performance of someone who reports to you is making it doubtful that your department will meet a critical deadline, but you know he just lost a child. Or what if you happen to know there is an imminent merger and as a result many senior leaders will be let go, but legally you can't make the knowledge public—and a colleague has told you she is about to buy a very expensive new home.

We find the writing of Joseph Badaracco helpful in giving people advice in working through the issues of everyday management. He recognizes the limitations of what he calls "inspirational ethics," the "just do the right thing" approach. As he says, "The inspirational approach offers little help with serious conflicts of responsibility. The truly difficult question is . . . : What to do when one clear right thing must be left undone in order to do another or when doing the right thing requires doing something wrong?"[6] Badaracco's work offers powerful and practical guidance, and we highly recommend his writing.

A CEO once asked us to facilitate a two-day retreat for his senior leadership. In addition to working on the company's strategic planning and helping build a cohesive team, he wanted us to facilitate a discussion of ethics. We initiated that by talking about the idea of gray areas. One participant pooh-poohed this, saying, "Everybody knows what the right thing to do is. People just don't always have the courage to do it." Others agreed with this idea.

Certainly that's true in many situations, but often it is not. We asked if there had been any ethical issues in the company's recent experience and were told this story. A proposal had gone out to several vendors, who all responded with their lowest prices, and the bidding was closed. Later, one vendor came back with a quote that was the lowest of all. We asked each participant in the discussion to write down one idea of what would have been the right thing to do. After collecting their answers we read out the responses. Not surprisingly, there was a range of opinions, and even after considerable discussion, the group could not come to consensus. Finding ethical clarity is rarely easy; ethics needs to be part of all discussions.

Promise Keeping: The Missing Link

Promise keeping is integrity writ large. Ellwood Oakley, an associate professor of legal studies at Georgia State University, has called it the missing link between codes of conduct and ethical action. He writes:

> *When the management team of a business does not routinely keep its promises to employees (as well as outside stakeholders), it will be difficult, if not impossible, to promote ethical conduct within the organization. How many of us would take comfort in a code of conduct that lauded ethical behavior when the very managers who had promulgated the code were ignoring promises they had made to us as employees?*[7]

We learn early that promises are sacred. If you are a parent, you will recognize the feeling of being caught when your children say, "But you promised!" We should all post on our walls and in our hearts the phrase "promise carefully." So often we don't. We've worked with many executives who were surprised by their 360-degree review feedback when they scored low on integrity. But the comments of others made clear that they had been cavalier with promises. As is often the case between parents and children, their false promises might have been misguided attempts not to disappoint. Someone asks hopefully, "Can you finish that software change by the end of the month?" And you agree, even though you know it will be difficult, or even impossible.

In 1995 we attended a talk by Frances Hesselbein (whom you met earlier in this book), former CEO of Girl Scouts of the USA and an eloquent proponent of character as the foundation of leadership. She radiates integrity and humility. Someone in the audience asked her, "What's the most important factor in your success as a leader?" Hesselbein hesitated and then answered, "Oh, I don't like that kind of question. But if I have to answer, I'd say this one thing: I've always tried never to break a promise."

THE IMPACT OF LEADERSHIP ON ORGANIZATIONAL CHARACTER

Leaders with character develop cultures of character that allow their organizations to withstand the kinds of pressures and dishonesty that undid HealthSouth and Enron. In this, senior leaders must take the lead. They are the setters and carriers of culture. In a recent survey of CEOs by the Southern Institute for Business and Professional Ethics, 99 percent of respondents said high ethical standards strengthen a company's competitive position in the long run.[8] And 97 percent agreed that the leader of an enterprise must also be the moral leader. Still, many executives don't appreciate their power as role models in this regard. Employees take their cues from superiors regarding how to conduct themselves. Written codes of conduct rarely carry as much weight as the visible actions of those in command.

Thus senior leaders have the ability and the obligation to create places where everyone feels responsible for the enterprise, both for its financial success and its ethical behavior. In other words, senior leaders must create cultures that nurture Leadership Character in everyone. They must build organizations that are leadership-friendly and character-friendly. In leadership-friendly organizations, people feel engaged and are unafraid to take risks. They feel empowered to make decisions and take the initiative. But what if senior leaders don't feel compelled to be moral leaders, to create cultures that promote speaking out and speaking up? It's up to each one of us to take responsibility for the ethics of whatever organization we're in, whether that's easy or not, and whether senior leaders have asked us to or not. It's a question, ultimately, of survival. Leadership-friendly organizations are resilient and adaptable, and in a world where conditions change rapidly, organizations that seek to flourish must be resilient.

The United Way of Metropolitan Atlanta is one organization that has successfully reimagined itself to meet changing conditions, and in the process it has built Leadership Character throughout its ranks. Its old business model was a familiar and staid one: an annual drive to raise money, which was then disbursed to fund a group of social service agencies. "The new purpose of United Way," explains Mark O'Connell, president, "was to be a community space where leaders, broadly defined, would identify the key community issues that needed attention. United Way would have a role in organizing the community to address and hopefully solve these problems. The fundraising campaign would become just one of our resources for that work. But to go from being a fund raiser to being a problem solver, our skills and mind-sets and ways of working together needed to be redefined."

O'Connell set this transformation in motion without realizing that even his leadership skills would have to be rebuilt. "As I put together a new leadership team," he recalls, "about half of the members were new. We called on outside experts to work with us to ensure that we started in lockstep, and that new and old didn't create a schism." The feedback from O'Connell's own 360-degree review at that time revealed many extreme strengths—and a few extreme weaknesses. "Mark is one of the strongest visionaries and most compelling leaders I have ever worked with," Bob says, "but he could be harsh and blaming with some of the people closest to him, and quick to cut off input."

O'Connell explains, "One of the new principles of our work, both within the organization and out in the community, was to build strengths from the inside out. That means valuing people's inputs, building off their strengths, seeing people as the assets they bring, not just as the deficits they have, which United Way social service work has historically done. We had to change that, so that in people in whom you might easily be able to identify weakness, you find the strengths. The same was true for our own staff. I myself needed to become more affirming, coaching, encouraging to develop the maternal side of me."

To ensure ongoing leadership development within the organization, an internal Community Building Institute was established. Fifteen people participate annually in this year-long learning experience, including not just professional members but receptionists, billing clerks, and maintenance staff. "This idea of seeing everybody as a player, valuing their different contributions, and then investing in them, building capacity in them, was new to us," says O'Connell.

The United Way's redefined mission required not only fresh skills but different values. "We needed measurability," O'Connell says, "evidence of organizational effectiveness. We needed accountability, to state what it was we were going to take on, and to gauge our degree of success. There was a value of inclusion. Community-based problems don't lend themselves to top-down approaches; we needed to be more of an inside-out organization, a bottom-up model. And we had to model that within the organization if we were going to live it in the community. Diversity, too, couldn't simply be an aspiration; it had to be a practice. We needed to move from being an organization that presumed it knew everything it needed to know about its work to being an organization that would learn. And we're still learning how to do the new work. Before, we had the arrogance of certainty. Now we have to be humble."

TOOLS FOR BUILDING YOUR INDIVIDUAL INTEGRITY

Integrity is like healthy moral muscle; it must be developed and strengthened, exercised and maintained in shape over time. These exercises, or ways of thinking, will help you build yours and keep it toned.

- **Develop a personal mission statement.** You can't act with integrity if you don't know what you are here in this life to accomplish, or if you aren't clear about the values you want to express as you do it. Ask yourself questions like, "Whom do I really admire?" and "How do I want to be remembered?" Draft a short statement about what you wish to accomplish and contribute. Review and revise it often.

- **Promise carefully.** Make only promises you can keep. Never over-promise and under-deliver; it's better to under-promise and over-deliver. Keep your promises.

- **Avoid exaggeration and embellishment.** People who aren't basically dishonest may do this because their self-confidence is shaky. If you find yourself prone to exaggeration, working on self-confidence might be what you need to do.

- **Embrace absolute honesty.** As you go through the day, think of what absolute honesty would really mean: never shading the truth, always admitting mistakes, never exaggerating, not talking about people behind their backs, not taking pens home from the office. Think of times when you have been less than thoroughly honest. Why did you shade the truth? To avoid conflict? Because it was the easy way out? How far are you right now from living an absolutely honest, open life?

- **Review your words.** Words are powerful and have a rippling effect. Be intentional and thoughtful about what you say, and about how you say it. Recall what you said in a recent meeting, for instance. Was it really honest and direct? Was it said with the best interest of the other person at heart, but also without holding back?

- **Use models of integrity.** Think of someone who has been important in your life, whom you respect for her or his commitment to values, and refer to your image of this person as a model of integrity. When you're faced with a difficult decision, ask yourself what that person would do. When evaluating how you have conducted yourself, consider how that person would have viewed you.

TOOLS FOR BUILDING YOUR ORGANIZATION'S INTEGRITY

In an organization with character, ethical issues can't be separate from the ordinary business at hand. Just as every decision is considered in light of financial implications, every decision must also be considered in light of ethical considerations. Ethical considerations should become as second-nature as financial ones. For organizations, just as for individuals, intentional focus makes that more likely to happen.

Organizations need constant monitoring and feedback from every member. You can't rely on whistle-blowing to protect your company. Whistle-blowers sometimes step forward in time to avert disaster, but too often their role is to help reveal already irreversible damage. How much better it is to create a trusting, respectful environment where people feel it's their duty to point out problems, conflicts of interest, and other ethical concerns as soon as they arise.

- **Create conversational tools.** Use your tools to make ethics a daily part of decision making. Designate an "ethics officer" in every meeting, to alert the group to possible concerns. In every process of decision making, make clear what the competing commitments are; in most situations, these are multiple and complex.

- **Increase transparency.** Teach all employees to understand financials; share the numbers; invite questions. Be as honest as possible about business plans, forecasts, and customer commitments. Increases in transparency also make it more likely that projects will be completed on time and within budget.

- **Create a feedback-rich environment.** Institute 360-degree review feedback for every manager, especially senior leadership. Find ways to give leaders regular verbal feedback. Try reverse mentoring, where a junior person mentors each senior executive, and require that the relationship be taken seriously. Administer regular employee and customer surveys, and distribute the results widely.

- **Get outside views.** When there is an ethical dilemma, find impartial resources. Call a trusted professional colleague, a consultant such as a professor of ethics, or colleagues from other departments.

- **Celebrate honesty and accountability.** Finally, make leaders who are completely honest and trustworthy your organization's heroes.

CHARACTER, LEADERSHIP, AND HEALING THE WORLD

Character is who you are at the core of your being, the complex of attributes that make you moral, righteous, dependable, and decent. Integrity is the fundamental quality of character: knowing your values, and being true to them at any cost. Leadership is the power to inspire and influence. It is not formal power or position, and anyone can find a way to express it.

Leadership Character is the initiative and courage to do what needs to be done in any situation, and the integrity and respect for others that inspire them to follow you toward the goal—a goal that, finally, you all decide together.

Leadership Character changes the question from "Why don't they . . . ?" to "What can I . . . ?"

Afterword

In closing, we would like to speak separately for a moment, straight from our hearts.

First, from Lyn: At the beginning of this book, we wrote about expectations: how we all are a mix of good and bad, and how what we expect, of ourselves and of others, creates what we get. Our job in life, as Abraham Lincoln said, is to bring forth "the better angels of our nature."

Years ago, I was moved by a Sunday school discussion about the idea that "God is watching us" and knows our every move. Many people would agree with that idea; but how many of us really live as though we are always on view before God? How different would our lives and world be if we all held that image in consciousness? The Hindus have a word of welcome, *nemaste,* which means, "I greet the God in you." I like to think of that. It reminds me that God is watching me through the eyes of everyone I encounter, whether that's across a conference table, at a dinner party, or even in the checkout line at the supermarket.

I always want to be seen as a person of character by the God in every person I meet.

And from Bob: Sometimes we meet people who see the God in us. For me, that was Frances Kinne, my humanities teacher when I was a sophomore in college. Even as a young professor, Dr. Kinne was one of the most effective and inspiring leaders I have ever encountered, and she remains the most profound example of leadership character I have ever met. Her enthusiasm was contagious. Her empathy and respect for her students, and her love of her subject, were complete; as a result, I never worked harder for any teacher.

Dr. Kinne went on to become dean of the fine arts department, and then the university's president. When she wanted to retire, the school couldn't bear to lose her counsel and so created the position of chancellor for her. Her integrity was unquestioned and her work ethic prodigious. I have never seen anyone who better balanced respect for others with unwavering responsibility. Her leadership elevated the stature of that obscure school, attracting sizable donations and impressive academic talent; during her tenure, new departments were founded, the physical campus expanded, and the university community greatly diversified. Years later, she is still the person I "consult" most often, in my head, when I confront an ethical challenge. I hope you, too, have someone in mind who embodies leadership character, with whom you can carry on that internal dialogue. Living an ethical life is hard enough; you don't have to attempt it all alone.

And from both of us, this treasured quote from Arthur Ashe, about building a better world:

"Start where you are, use what you have, do what you can."

Notes

Introduction

[1] Michael Skapinker, "Can Business Be Both Caring and Profitable?" *Financial Times* (27 October 2003), Management Special Report, 1.

[2] Bill George, "Interview with Bill George" (15 October 2003) *http://www. dupree.gatech.edu/news_room/news/2003/impact/george/files/george_Q_A.pdf.*

Chapter 1

[1] William Drath, "Changing Our Minds About Leadership," *Issues and Observations,* Center for Creative Leadership, 16, no. 1 (1996).

[2] David Cooperrider, "Positive Image, Positive Action: The Affirmative Basis of Organizing" in *Appreciative Inquiry: An Emerging Direction for Organization Development,* David L. Cooperrider, Peter F. Sorensen Jr., Therese F. Yaeger, and Diana Whitney, eds. (Champaign, IL: Stipes Publishing, 2001).

[3] M. Snyder, E. Tanke, & E. Berscheid, "Social Perception and Interpersonal Behavior: On the Self-Fulfilling Nature of Social Stereotypes," *Journal of Personality and Social Psychology* 35 (1977), 656–666.

[4] Robert Rosenthal & Leonore Jacobson, *Pygmalion in the Classroom* (New York: Holt, Rinehart and Winston, 1968).

[5] Sigal G. Barsade, Andrew J. Ward, et al., "To Your Heart's Content: A Model of Affective Diversity in Top Management Teams," *Administrative Science Quarterly* (1 December 2000), 802–836, as reported in Daniel Goleman, *Primal Leadership* (Boston: Harvard Business School Publishing, 2002), pp. 14–15.

[6] Jennifer M. George & Kennety Bettenhausen, "Understanding Prosocial Behavior, Sales Performance, and Turnover: A Group-Level Analysis in Service Context," *Journal of Applied Psychology* 75 (1990), 698–709, as reported in Goleman, *Primal Leadership,* 16.

[7] John Schaubroeck & Deryl E. Merritt, "Divergent Effects of Job Control on Coping with Work Stressors: The Key Role of Self-Efficacy," *Academy of Management Journal* 40 (1997), 738–754. See also Fred Luthans, "Positive Organizational Behavior: Developing and Managing Psychological Strengths," *Academy of Management Executive 16* (2002), 57–75.

[8] Emmett C. Murphy, *Leadership IQ: A Personal Development Process Based on a Scientific Study of a New Generation of Leaders* (New York: Wiley, 1996).

[9] Frances Hesselbein, "The How-to-Be Leader," *Leader of the Future,* Frances Hesselbein, Marshall Goldsmith, & Richard Beckhard, eds. (San Francisco: Jossey-Bass, 1996).

Chapter 2

[1] For a thorough discussion of the Ohio State and University of Michigan studies, see chapters 23 and 24 of Bernard M. Bass, *Bass & Stogdill's Handbook of Leadership* (New York: Free Press, 1990).

[2] Robert Kaplan & Robert Kaiser, "The Forceful and Enabling Polarity: A Fresh Look at an Old Distinction," presented in a practitioner forum at the 16th annual conference of the Society of Industrial and Organizational Psychology, San Diego, CA (April 2001).

Chapter 3

[1] Ram Charan & Jerry Useem, "Why Companies Fail," *Fortune* (27 May 2002), 52.

[2] Gus Pagonis, "The Work of a Leader," *Harvard Business Review* (November–December 1992), 120.

[3] Jean Leslie & Ellie Van Velsor. *A Look at Derailment Today: North America and Europe.* CCL No. 169. (Greensboro, NC: Center for Creative Leadership, 1996).

[4] Daniel Goleman, "Leadership That Gets Results," *Harvard Business Review* (March–April 2000), 81.

[5] Daniel Goleman, "What Makes a Leader," *Harvard Business Review* (November–December 1998) 94.

[6] Gallup study reported in Marcus Buckingham and Curt Coffman, *First Break All the Rules—What the World's Greatest Managers Do Differently* (New York: Simon & Schuster, 1999).

[7] Goleman, *Primal Leadership*, 5.

[8] Goleman, "What Makes a Leader," 97.

[9] Peter Senge, *The Fifth Discipline: The Art and Practice of the Learning Organization* (New York: Doubleday, 1990).

[10] Jim Trelease, *The Read-Aloud Handbook,* 5th ed. (New York: Penguin Books, 2001).

Chapter 4

[1] Jack Welch, quoted in Alan Webber, "What's so New About the New Economy?" *Harvard Business Review* (January–February 1993), 41.

[2] Maxie Maultsby, *Help Yourself to Happiness* (New York: Albert Ellis Institute, 1995).

Chapter 5

[1] Chris Argyris, "Teaching Smart People How to Learn," *Harvard Business Review* (May–June 1991), 100.

[2] Arbinger Institute, *Leadership and Self-Deception* (San Francisco: Berrett-Koehler, 2002).

[3] For an earlier discussion of David McClelland's work, see his classic 1976 article (with David Burnham), "Power Is the Great Motivator," reprinted in *Harvard Business Review* (January 2003), 117–26, or his 1975 book, *Power: The Inner Experience* (New York: Irvington, 1975). Leadership styles and climate were discussed in the early work of Rensis Likert, *The Human Organization: Its Management and Value* (New York: McGraw-Hill, 1967).

[4] See Goleman, "Leadership That Gets Results," for a thorough description of the styles.

[5] Goleman, "Leadership That Gets Results," 83.

[6] Goleman, "Leadership That Gets Results," 82.

[7] Goleman, "Leadership That Gets Results," 82.

---

[8] Daniel Goleman, *Primal Leadership*, 64–65.
[9] Goleman, *Primal Leadership*, 65.
[10] Goleman, "Leadership That Gets Results," 87.

Chapter 6

[1] Bill Fleming & Brent Holland, "Flawed Interpersonal Strategies and Multi-Source Feedback," paper presented at the 16th annual conference of the Society of Industrial and Organizational Psychology, Toronto, ONT (April 2002), 5.
[2] Fleming & Holland, "Flawed Interpersonal Strategies," 5. See also Robert Hogan, "Trouble at the Top: Causes and Consequences of Managerial Incompetence," *Consulting Psychology Journal* 46 (1994).
[3] Victor Rozek, "Caring Leadership–the Leader as Servant," *The Four Hundred* (3 March 2003). [Online] Available at http://www.midrangerserver.com/tfh/tfh 030303 story05.html.
[4] For an understanding of Greenleaf's views, first articulated in the 1970s, see Robert Greenleaf, Larry Spears, & Stephen Covey, *Servant Leadership: A Journey into the Nature of Legitimate Power and Greatness* (New York: Paulist Press, 2002).

Chapter 7

[1] Kaplan & Kaiser, "The Forceful and Enabling Polarity," 2.
[2] Kaplan & Kaiser, "The Forceful and Enabling Polarity," 2.
[3] Gary Hamel, "Waking Up IBM," *Harvard Business Review* (July–August 2000), 140.
[4] Hamel, "Waking Up IBM," 146.
[5] Robert Kegan & Lisa Lahey, *How the Way We Talk Can Change the Way We Work* (San Francisco: Jossey-Bass, 2001).
[6] Kegan & Lahey, 2001, 31.
[7] Both Blanchard & Hersey have written books describing the theory, and there are numerous descriptions available on the Internet. For one description, see Kenneth Blanchard & Patricia Zigarmi, *Leadership and the One Minute Manager: Increasing Effectiveness Through Situational Leadership* (New York: William Morrow, 1999).

Chapter 8

[1] "Persons of the Year—2002," *Time Magazine* (30 December 2002).

Chapter 9

[1] Noel Tichy & Ram Charan, "Speed, Simplicity, and Self Confidence: An Interview with Jack Welch," *Harvard Business Review* (September–October 1989), 112–120.
[2] Patti Waldmeir, *Anatomy of a Miracle: The End of Apartheid and the Birth of the New South Africa*, (Piscataway, NJ: Rutgers University Press, 1998), 89.
[3] Waldmeir, *Anatomy of a Miracle*, 89.

Chapter 10

[1] Martin Linsky & Ronald Heifetz, *Leadership on the Line* (Boston: Harvard Business School Press), 53.

[2] Linsky & Heifetz, *Leadership on the Line*, 54.

[3] Drath, "Changing Our Minds About Leadership," 2.

[4] Robert Kegan, *In Over Our Heads: The Mental Demands of Modern Life* (Boston: Harvard University Press, 1996).

[5] Karl Kuhnert & Keith Eigel, "Knowing How to Know Leaders: Leadership Level and Executive Effectiveness," Unpublished manuscript (2004).

[6] Kuhnert & Eigel, "Knowing Leaders," 5.

[7] Barry Johnson, *Polarity Management: Identifying and Managing Unsolvable Problems* (Amherst, MA: Human Resource Development Press, 1997).

[8] Arie de Geus, *The Living Company* (Boston: Harvard University Press, 1997).

Chapter 11

[1] Tony Simons, "The High Cost of Lost Trust," *Harvard Business Review* (September 2002), 18–19.

[2] "After Enron: The Ideal Corporation," *BusinessWeek* (26 August 2002).

[3] George Lakoff, *Moral Politics: How Liberals and Conservatives Think* (Chicago: University of Chicago Press, 2002).

[4] Ken Wilber, *A Brief History of Everything,* (Boston: Shambhala Publications, 2001), 3.

[5] Kenneth Cloke & Joan Goldsmith, *The End of Management and the Rise of Organizational Democracy* (San Francisco: Jossey-Bass, 2002).

[6] Joseph L. Badaracco, Jr., *Defining Moments* (Boston: Harvard Business School Press, 1997), 6.

[7] Ellwood F. Oakley, "Codes of Conduct and Promise Keeping," Good Business 2, no. 3 (2003), http://www.southerninstitute.org/Resources-GoodBusiness-Content (25).htm (3rd/4th Quarter 2003).

[8] Southern Institute for Business and Professional Ethics, "The Survey of Georgia CEOs on Business Ethics" (April 2002), <http://www.southerninstitute.org/Surveyfr.htm>.

Index

DATE DUE